Music Therapy in Adoption and Trauma

of related interest

Seven Core Issues in Adoption and Permanency
A Comprehensive Guide to Promoting Understanding and Healing in Adoption, Foster Care, Kinship Families and Third Party Reproduction
Sharon Kaplan Roszia and Allison Davis Maxon
Foreword by Deborah N. Silverstein, MSW
ISBN 978 1 78592 823 9
eISBN 978 1 78450 930 9

Music Therapy and Autism Across the Lifespan
A Spectrum of Approaches
Edited by Henry Dunn, Elizabeth Coombes, Emma Maclean, Helen Mottram and Josie Nugent
Foreword by Adam Ockelford
ISBN 978 1 78592 311 1
eISBN 978 1 78450 622 3

The Simple Guide to Attachment Difficulties in Children
What They Are and How to Help
Betsy de Thierry
ISBN 978 1 78592 639 6
eISBN 978 1 78592 640 2

Creative Therapies for Complex Trauma
Helping Children and Families in Foster Care, Kinship Care or Adoption
Edited by Anthea Hendry and Joy Hasler
Foreword by Colwyn Trevarthen
ISBN 978 1 78592 005 9
eISBN 978 1 78450 242 3

MUSIC THERAPY in Adoption and Trauma

THERAPY THAT MAKES A DIFFERENCE AFTER PLACEMENT

Joy Gravestock
Foreword by Helen Odell-Miller

Jessica Kingsley Publishers
London and Philadelphia

First published in Great Britain in 2021 by Jessica Kingsley Publishers
An Hachette Company

2

Copyright © Joy Gravestock 2021
Foreword copyright © Helen Odell-Miller 2021

All rights reserved. No part of this publication may be reproduced, stored in a retrieval system, or transmitted, in any form or by any means without the prior written permission of the publisher, nor be otherwise circulated in any form of binding or cover other than that in which it is published and without a similar condition being imposed on the subsequent purchaser.

A CIP catalogue record for this title is available from the
British Library and the Library of Congress

ISBN 978 1 78592 523 8
eISBN 978 1 78450 912 5

Printed and bound in the United States by Integrated Books International

Jessica Kingsley Publishers' policy is to use papers that are natural, renewable and recyclable products and made from wood grown in sustainable forests. The logging and manufacturing processes are expected to conform to the environmental regulations of the country of origin.

Jessica Kingsley Publishers
Carmelite House
50 Victoria Embankment
London EC4Y 0DZ

www.jkp.com

*This book is dedicated with gratitude to Lily and Jilly
Who have taught me so much
About how to love
By their sharing of lived experience*

Contents

	Foreword by Helen Odell-Miller	9
	Prologue: Lived Experience and Sense-Making Informing Music Therapy in the Adoption Community	19
1.	The Relevance of Music Therapy for the Adoption Community	29
2.	The Contemporary Adoption Process in the UK: The Impact of Process on Music Therapy.	45
3.	Sense-Making of Lived Experience: A Theoretical Approach .	61
4.	Accessing Music Therapy: The Adoption Support Fund	79
5.	Referral Presentations: A Needs-Led Approach for Diverse Issues	93
6.	A Needs-Led Music Therapy Approach: Listening To Lived Experience	107
7.	How Music Therapy Supports Adoptions in Difficulty	123
8.	An Adoption Narrative Informing Music Therapy	141
9.	Resonances of the Music Therapist's Self in Intersubjective Relating: The Significance of Therapists' Lived Experiences of Adoption	161
10.	Lily: Learning from Lived Experience.	177
11.	Co-Constructing Future Practice with the Adoption Community	195
	Appendix 1	205

Appendix 2	207
References	211
Subject Index	217
Author Index	221

Foreword

HELEN ODELL-MILLER

Writing this in the middle of the pandemic COVID-19, during a full lockdown, I am reminded of the likely experiences of an outsider. For many people, the familiar comforts of life are curtailed, and face to face contact with family friends and loved ones has also decreased and in some cases ceased. As outsiders looking in, often through a screen, many people are reporting feelings of abandonment, loneliness and of severed contact with those they love. Intimacy, and the close warm physical proximity with loved ones can be temporarily lost. In this book, the experience of the often traumatised abandoned baby, child, or young person now adopted; is powerfully described, and uniquely the place of music and music therapy is explored.

Music therapy pays attention to how the therapist and participant in music therapy make music, and the unique contribution music therapy makes to this relationship is explored throughout the book. Joy Gravestock vividly shows us; through case examples and her own understanding of the work; how reparation of ruptured family relationships can occur through the evocation of early 'conversations' which may have taken place between baby and birth mother. Making music in the music therapy room can resemble and recreate the motherese or protoconversation, which may have been lost through separating the child from birth parents. Each case example is unique and there is no direct model or solution for the work, but rather, the author draws attention to the importance of paying overt attention to the likely losses and family related trauma that could be played out within families who have adopted children.

The many facets of the family experiences through adoption are explored, providing in depth insights into the adoption process, both from an experiential political and clinical perspective. Strikingly, whilst knowledge, research and understanding of the adoption process has developed in the last two decades, and attachment theory is more widely known about in the field, it often falls to the therapist, (in this case the music therapist), to facilitate insights within a family; of how traumatic early separation can be.

Strikingly, the book addresses many issues head on, for example cultural, political, psychological and practice based ethical dilemmas previously not articulated from a music therapy perspective. Whilst reading the book, one aspect of the value of music therapy stands out, which is so often spoken about in definitions of music therapy, but here is authentically realised—that of the 'non-verbal' qualities possible in the music therapy process. There are emotions and thoughts which are unspeakable, or too painful to be put into words. Through musical expression in music therapy, these can be experienced by both therapist and participants, and lead to relief, interpretation, understanding, new meaning and acceptance.

For readers who are music therapists, participants within music therapy (potential, current, or past), professional social workers, therapists, allied health professionals, nurses, medical staff and all members of society; curiosity to understand more will be stimulated. The lived experience of people who have experienced adoption is valued and explored, including through the author's own experience. This is both moving, courageous and adds to the understanding and training of music therapists, as well as to all those who may find themselves relating to children who are adopted.

Improvisational music therapy, where the music therapist works through their own instrument, musically 'in the moment' with the participant, sometimes leads to a new understanding of the nature of the child's needs, and history. Subsequently, musical interactions can facilitate new understanding and meaning. The book includes examples of both receptive and active music therapy approaches, showing how listening and paying attention to the sounds of the other can enable families to relate in new ways. Similarly, literally reaching a pure form of attention to others, is repeatedly demonstrated through interactive music -making, showing developing respect for personal space, pace, affect, styles of relating, emotional needs. Ultimately this can lead to increased loving relationships within the family, or within children or young people themselves, through the music therapy process.

I invite readers to go further, to discover how new musical thinking built on relational theory, integrated with music therapy approaches appropriate for family work and work with people, especially children who are adopted; unfolds.

Acknowledgments

To the following people, without whom writing would have been impossible, and who shared the lived experience of bringing a book to being.

Nick Gravestock, for keeping life sustained in every way.

Frances O'Brien, for holding on to hope and showing me the value of attachment based, trauma informed, relational therapy.

Christine Atkinson, for supervision that is always both robust and kind.

Thea Abbot and David Van Edwards, for first suggesting that this book and a PhD might even be possible.

Friends/colleagues at Coram Adoption Shepshed, for trusting my work in the early days, with special thanks to Corrine and Anne.

Friends/colleagues in Leicestershire, Derbyshire, and Nottinghamshire Local authorities, for continuing to value the work by sending referrals to music therapy. With special thanks to Gail Newby for her understanding and valuing of the work, and endless patience with me.

Professor Brendan Stone, for introducing me to the concepts of lived experience and sense-making as academic paradigms. Also Dr Anthony Williams and Dr Chris Wood, for being a PhD team who constantly cause me to interrogate my work.

And to all the people who have become family during this journey.

Dr Pawan Randev and Dr Puneet Srivastava and the Derby Royal Hospital Rheumatology Team, for keeping my body going so my mind could do this writing!

Preface

This book has come into being as a result of my experiences of working as a music therapist within what is known as the 'adoption community', and also through having my own identity as a member of that adoption community. My personal position undoubtedly informs my therapeutic position and work. I have been privileged as a therapist to hear many adoption narratives, to witness and explore histories of trauma that have led to adoption, to learn how families have come to be joined together, and to share the pain of possible adoption breakdowns, while also seeing hopeful new possibilities for relating emerge in music therapy. I have learned about the desire of individuals and families within the adoption community to share their stories so that professionals can support them in a needs-led manner.

To this end, anonymized case studies are shared throughout the text with consent from individuals and families. Chapter 8 explores adoption-specific themes described entirely through case narratives, and Chapter 10 offers an in-depth analysis of a single long-term music therapy intervention. This book aims then to describe the evolution of the sort of music therapy people in the adoption community have found helpful, and which they would advocate for others.

The adoption community is a term used to describe the shared networks of individual lives that are connected by the experience of adoption, in some way. Membership of this community is gained by being either an adoptee or an adoptive parent/grandparent/relative. Being part of a community of people who share an adoption identity helps to lessen feelings of difference, shame and isolation that can arise from the experiences of being adopted, or being an adopter. As one adopter states, 'Being part of the adoption community means I get to be with other parents who really get what it's like. I can cry, laugh, share stories freely, without feeling judged. My children get to be with other adopted children and know they are not on their own. It is so important to know there is a whole community out there like us.' Or as one child put it simply, 'I meet and play with friends who understand what I've been through.' In a wider sense, the adoption community also includes adoption professionals with extensive experience who provide online resources, live access to experts, conferences, and activity days where families can be together and know that they all share the lived experience of being either adopted or an adopter.

The personal lived experience of professionals working in the adoption community is considered valuable because this community has really learned from the lived experiences of its members, and continues to do so. As such, it can be somewhat wary of those who do not have this lived experience telling those who do have it how to be! This then is why it has been imperative for me to centre the writing of this book on the expressed hopes for music therapy practice which the adoption community articulate.

I have myself been at various times a service user, a client, a therapist, an adoption panel member, a researcher, and here now an author. I am inevitably involved in sense-making of my own lived experience, alongside that of my clients, as we are piecing together experiences and theoretical concepts to form an approach that is specific to the needs expressed by individual adoptees/adopters. I could not have attempted any of this work without belonging to the community, and having my professional view (rooted as it is in my processed lived experience) given credence by the community.

Scant attention has been given to the lived experience of the music therapist who chooses to work with a client group who have some similarity of experience to herself, and how this might resonate in intersubjective relationships with her clients. Yet such lived experience is significant to the trajectory of our work, either recognized or unconscious. As music therapists, our own experiences can, if not known and explored as much as is possible in our own therapy and supervision, cause us to over-identify with our clients, or to project our material onto them. To minimize the risk of this happening, it is imperative we stay alive to our own narratives and needs. However, despite such potential pitfalls, I still believe that the employment of professionals with established knowledge who also have personal lived experience of adoption is important and extremely useful when working with an at times delicate and fractured community. It has most use when individual professionals can work together with other members of the adoption community who have differing lived experiences, so that the process of making sense of client's presentations has checks and balances.

I have spoken with others who are fearful that their own membership of a community might exclude them from practising within it. Also, some music therapists describe it being hard to enter adoption work because they lack experience of adoption and don't know where to get it from. To such I would offer hope, and suggest that openness and authenticity with those who employ music therapists is imperative, to help us to negotiate potential areas of difficulty.

Many of the clients described in this book had experienced a whole gamut of treatments and interventions before being referred to music therapy. Often they would describe feeling labelled and blamed in the process. This is why in this text (as in my therapeutic practice) I deliberately move away from diagnostic type descriptions or 'labels' and towards relational descriptions. I choose not to describe clients' presentations in terms of any type of 'attachment disorder' or other diagnostic category they might have accrued. Many adopted people describe struggling with being given an attachment disorder diagnosis because of the implication that *they* are somehow 'disordered' or 'damaged'. It can be a relief, therefore, to lay this label down, at least for a while, in the music therapy space. Throughout this book, I am not then advocating a method to treat a 'disorder', but instead offer descriptions of a music therapy approach that considers the meaning of traumatic material as it is played out in relationships, and how this might be understood and turned towards relational change. I have come to understand the difficulties occurring in adoptive families attending music therapy as disorders of relationship on which trauma has negatively impacted. Music happens in what I describe as 'the spaces between relationships', and is therefore a well-placed modality for holding and working with relational material.

Throughout this text, I use the term 'we' to describe myself and other music therapists collectively. However, this book is also written for adoption specialists (who I hope will gain some insight into the process of music therapy) and members of the adoptive community themselves (who may be enabled to articulate further the sorts of help and therapy they desire).

In addition to my dedication (mentioning individuals who have specifically been significant to me during the process of the conception and writing of this book), I also acknowledge my own local adoption community (who have been happy to discuss and argue with my work) as well as all of those whose experiences and stories have contributed in no small way to shaping my practice today.

Prologue

LIVED EXPERIENCE AND SENSE-MAKING INFORMING MUSIC THERAPY IN THE ADOPTION COMMUNITY

Lived experience

In 2017, my PhD supervisor, Professor Brendan Stone (Sheffield University), was the first person to bring to my awareness two academic concepts or philosophies that have become integral to my research, and subsequently to the writing of this book: lived experience and sense-making. First, lived experience is a term that has arisen from qualitative research and which describes a representation and understanding of either a researcher, or research subjects, human experiences, choices, and options, and how these factors influence our perception of knowledge. In phenomenological research, lived experiences are essentially the main object of study, and the goal of such research is not necessarily to understand lived experience as fact, but to determine the understandable meaning (or indeed meanings) of such experience/s.

This notion resonates in my work with adoptive families who, when they come to music therapy, might have various members with very different lived experiences of the same events. As music therapists, we are not tasked with uncovering who in the family has the 'true' experience, and persuading the others to that view. Rather, we explore what differing meaning individuals are making of their experience and how such meaning-making impacts on family members relating together. The academic value placed on explorations of lived experience is helpful to music therapists, as with our clients we construct ways to make sense of, and therapeutically hold, the experiences brought to music therapy, without privileging one person's experience over another's.

The lived experience of adoptees and adopters is at the centre of my understanding throughout this book of what it means to both adopt and be adopted. It is also at the locus of any theoretical stance and methodology describing how music therapists might practice in order to support this family form.

Lived experience impacting the adoption community

The adoption community has for many years seriously valued the lived experiences of its members. The depth of listening to lived experience is indicated by significant changes to practice. An example of such change is when the lived experiences of adoptees from minority ethnic groups impacted the way adoption placements were made.

In the 1960s, the idea of a white family adopting a child from a different, minority ethnic group was not subject to the same considerations and critique that we have today. Only as these children grew up and had profound experiences of racism and struggled with additional issues pertaining to their sense of cultural identity did many members of the community begin to learn that this was not best practice for the future psychological wellbeing and self-integration of the adoptee. Jackie Kay's (1991) book of poems, *The Adoption Papers*, tells the story of a dual heritage child being adopted into a white Scottish family – her own lived experience. Although she found love and a strong sense of self within her placement, this was coupled with immense pain, loss and identity confusion, all of which she articulates in the poetry. Adoption professionals heard similar stories from adult adoptees who said that racial and cultural identity was core to developing a sense of self for an adopted child. Now, as part of the 'matching process' (where decisions are made about which children are matched with which parents) at adoption panels, ethnicity and cultural matching is seen as imperative. Panels will try to match as closely as possible so that a child can grow up connected to their birth culture, and not alienated from it. Race and culture provide just one example of many where difficult lived experience changed practice.

Sense-making and lived experience

If my own work, rooted in the lived experience of adopted people in music therapy, was to impact the adoption community in a similarly meaningful way, I first had to engage in a process described to me (Stone 2017) as 'sense-making' of their lived experience. Sense-making is a theory that comes originally from social psychology (Weick 1995). It suggests that telling and hearing narratives within families can have lasting effects and create enduring values, impressions, fears and beliefs. The content and process of family storytelling link to mental, physical and relational health.

Adoptive families came to music therapy with certain narratives of how life had been to date and continued to construct and reconstruct stories together about how they understood their reactions and responses. In the course of my attempts to provide a framework for thinking about adoption, I first had to hear the stories of families which shed light on their relational communications, and the functions of such communications. With every family I have worked with, it has been imperative to go through a process of hearing their story, witnessing the trauma and then beginning together to evolve new sense-making through music therapy.

Sharing in sense-making is a way for people (in this case, multiple members of any adoptive family) to think retrospectively together about their varied and often seemingly contrasting, contravening or even oppositional lived experiences. In a process of sense-making within adoptive families, different individuals might be enabled to think together about the other's experience, and why this experience might be as valid as their own, even if two experiences seemed to be describing apparent differences.

Challenges to the perceived value of lived experience

I realized that for some time in my work with adoptees and adoptive families, I had been unknowingly drawing on theories of both lived experience and sense-making. However, the somewhat simplistic idea of any and all lived experience being valuable to the adoption community is one that needed some thinking about and challenging.

For example, the guidance for adoption panels has for many years stated explicitly that every panel must include both an adoptee and an adoptive parent. This guidance is underpinned by a core belief that people with lived experience of adoption have 'something to bring' to the panel, yet what this 'something' should be is not made explicit. A challenge to those who convene the panel might be to ask them to define *how* they think a panel member's personal lived experience of being an adoptee or adoptive parent will be of use to the panel and those with whom the panel work. There is a danger that lip service is given to the idea of the value of experience for its own sake, which results in just ticking a box that states the experience is present in the room. A single individual's experience is only one example of lived experience, and as such cannot become a template or a definitive view, nor should it be a standard by which to judge another's (different) experience. One adoptee/adopter does not equate to all adoptees/adopters, and there is a danger also that individuals engaged in work because of their identity become categorized by this single status. What contribution might members bring to the panel when perhaps their own lived experience has been negative, and therefore could put a negative 'spin' on decision making?

Lived experience and sense-making incorporated: first steps to an adoption music therapy

When I began working in the field of adoption specifically as a music therapist, I already had over a decade of experience of specialist adoption practice working within Child and Adolescent Mental Health Services (CAMHS). I could therefore draw on a range of well-established methods and resources already being used in adoption. Previous training in attachment and family therapy meant I was able to make some sense of the complex relational dynamics adoptive families brought to music therapy. Additional earlier trainings in psychoanalysis helped me think about the internal worlds of both adopted children and adoptive parents, and how this might influence relationships as they played out in family placements. Despite my experience, it became obvious that any 'method' I might have previously advocated needed to be adapted and re-thought both in light of the children's and families' narratives that emerged time and again in the therapeutic work, and in the music that was played (or not played) between clients, their families, and me.

I had not necessarily intended to return to the field of adoption when I qualified as a music therapist, but the adoption community called me back! Colleagues I had previously worked with contacted me wanting to explore what music therapy might offer to families in complex adoption situations (such as threat of breakdown later in placement, or issues with 'hard to place' children pre-placement). I had a long-established contact with a local branch of a national charitable adoption service, as well as having contact and previously established relationships with locality social services teams, especially post-adoption, across the East and West Midlands. I had previously sat on an East Midlands adoption panel, with a dual identity as a therapist and someone with personal experience of adoption. When I qualified and was once again available to work, another East Midlands adoption panel recruited me, for the same experiences I would bring to the panel.

Colleagues locally have been very keen to think with me about how music therapy might be provided to adoptive children, young people, and their families. Initially we agreed to focus on referrals of adoptive families who were struggling to stay together. We hypothesized that a powerful dynamic was being played out in what were defined as 'failing placements' at 'risk of breakdown'. These families who felt as if they were failing often were referred for music therapy as a last resort, and usually were described as 'struggling with attachment disorder'. Attachment difficulties tended to be largely viewed as something residing in the child, who might somehow be 'fixed' through music therapy. It was my first working hypothesis as a music therapist then that so-called attachment disorder might exist less as a 'thing' in its own right, residing like an illness in a child, and instead might be thought of more helpfully as a difficulty in relationship that existed in the relational space between adoptive parent and child, the very site of the 'acting out' of trauma-related behaviour.

I proposed in early papers (Gravestock 2012) that it was at the interface of their internal worlds where children and parents were struggling to make sense of the other's lived experience, and the impact such experience might be having. Adoptive parents would have their own internal working model (about their own history of being parented, and their own expectations of child rearing), which came into conflict with their child's internal working model (about their own early life experience). These two internal worlds would collide in the relational space between child and adopter, resulting in adoption crises and the threat of total placement breakdown. It was not then so much a matter of music therapy 'fixing' traumatized adoptees, but rather working *with the relationships and their genesis* (which may involve work with the child alone, parents alone, or family all together). Two social worker colleagues especially had a personal interest in music and believed in the power of music as an intervention. They had valued my work previously within adoption, and trusted my experience and knowledge of the subject. They were happy to send the first referrals to me as we began together to engage in sense-making about what music therapy might offer to adoption placements in crisis.

Gathering theory and evolving an approach

I have endeavoured to write this book, as indeed I have developed my therapeutic practice, using the principle described below by Winnicott (Phillips 2007, p.16) as a gradual gathering and accumulating:

> What happens is that I gather this and that, here and there, settle down to clinical experience, form my own theories, and then, last of all, interest myself to see where I stole what. Perhaps this is as good a method as any.

It is the best description I have found for my own processes first as therapist, then as researcher, and now as author. It seems to me now that I initially came to work as a music therapist in the field of adoption probably only possessing 'this and that' to help me make sense of the work.

The task then began of 'forming my own theories' (in Winnicott's words) and I was led to diverse sources that helped me think. My PhD research took me into the realms of other creative expressive therapies, to developments in contemporary psychoanalysis, to attachment theory informed by neuroscience, to relational psychoanalysis and relational music therapy, and even to philosophy. I revisited core theorists of attachment, such as Bowlby and Winnicott, who describe the significance of the very earliest days of life, and the enduring impact this time can have on a developing baby. Many of my descriptions of the work initially were 'stolen' from such early writers, as they seemed to offer the best descriptors for what I saw week on week in the music therapy room. Daniel Stern's (1998) writing and video analysis also seemed to come alive in front of me, and gave me a sense that the very early life experiences of rejection and abandonment, or physical, emotional and sexual abuse that adopted children had internalized were very real in their 'here-and-now' relating with their adoptive families. Attunement that had been lost to adopted children in early life was impacting now on their capacity to risk and trust and relate within new families.

Having presented my work at conferences and written papers, I was being asked how I 'did' music therapy, and why was it 'working' (in that no family had experienced disruption to the point of breakdown). This became the impetus for my PhD, where I could explore in depth all of the ideas that contributed to my practice.

As I witnessed painful stories of loss and trauma from adopted children, young people and adults, I also became intimately acquainted with the reality of the lived experience of secondary trauma. Parents who (for the most part) only ever wanted to provide a loving home for their children seemed to find it impossible to do so. Early traumatic experience that children had known (perhaps even when they were just days old) was nonetheless powerful in its ability to affect current relating. Adopters, too, came with complex internal worlds which were also manifest in new family relating, often unhelpfully. Yet, in making music with them, I could see how what Trevarthen (2009) describes as 'communicative musicality' had the potential to provide opportunities for new relational styles to emerge and be experimented with.

I never set out to become either an author or a researcher. It is the therapeutic work itself that has led to these other roles being assumed. As I began to develop my own approach for working with families, I had to listen deeply to what their lived experience shared stories of broken relationships were saying. The approach I had developed to that point did seem to help, but the depth of difficulty and distress that was presented required more thinking if I was to incorporate the lived experience of the adoption community into any future work.

Both my own therapy and clinical supervision not only helped me work with my own lived experience but also directed me to find theoretical underpinnings for the work I did (and I acknowledge their holding of me throughout). I have engaged in extensive further trauma and attachment training which included new thinking around attachment (especially the growing field of neurobiology resulting from the impact of functional magnetic resonance imaging (fMRi) and neuroscience findings). Additional development came from various fields of verbal psychotherapy, especially new developments in contemporary relational psychoanalytic thinking about trauma and attachment. I began to describe my music therapy methodology of working with adoptive families as being attachment and trauma informed, and specifying that I was utilizing aspects of relational psychoanalytic thinking. As there was no evidence of a solid body of research in this specific practice modality to uncover, my supervisor suggested that maybe I should be providing some! She encouraged me to write and present my work, which was well received. Mention was then made then of turning 'in the field' work into a formally researched PhD. Such research is ongoing at the time of writing this book, and it is my hope that both the academic research and this more practice-based book might be of use to other music therapists and the families they encounter. I also hope it will be more widely read by other creative arts therapists, as well as other expert professionals in the field (such as social workers) involved in adoption work and making decisions about therapies provided. Finally, I hope families themselves will read it and offer feedback so that as music therapists we can continually evolve the sense-making of the work we ourselves do by listening to how such work is perceived and understood in the adoption community.

It is then this 'gathering' of ideas that I share here within this book. I share Winnicott's optimism that 'perhaps this is as good a method as any'. It has been difficult to formalize my thinking as a method or 'model' as such because when working with lived experience, we are always required to come to each therapeutic situation afresh and to be client-led. This means that sometimes we might have to drop our model because a particular client is communicating something new for us to consider that lies outside the usual parameters of our thinking. We may have to borrow from other therapeutic paradigms that might have something to say to us. If a client does not fit into the 'box' that usually holds our work, instead of trying to make them fit we might actually have to go and find a different box... I think it is incumbent on us as music therapists working with adoption trauma to be alive to every moment and to allow our clients' own creativity to lead the way. Music therapy, though, happens within music, which is always difficult to translate into words. Adopted children and their families have used the music therapy room, the frame of therapy, the instruments, and their relationship with me as therapist to first communicate their early life and trauma experience, and later to experiment with new relational possibilities. I hope that by sharing a collaborative and co-creative approach within this book that the lived experience of these children and families, and the sense-making we have together done, will provide an approach for others either doing this work themselves or supporting it.

Chapter 1

The Relevance of Music Therapy for the Adoption Community

Usually the first question I am asked by either an enquiring parent or a professional who is considering referring a child or a family to music therapy is, 'Why exactly is music therapy thought to be a useful therapeutic modality specifically for working with adoptive families?'

The simplest answer is that music therapy is first and foremost a non-verbal modality. As all music therapists know, music does not have to rely on words for its efficacy. Indeed, part of the difficulty of explaining how and why music therapy 'works' is that of translating what happens in music into verbal language. However, many children and families who are referred for music therapy have already been offered various other types of verbal interventions for the difficulties they present with, and usually such interventions have been deemed 'unsuccessful'. Music therapy might then be the 'afterthought therapy', rather than a first choice, in many cases, once families have found themselves unable to engage verbally.

Part of the difficulty in engaging with verbal therapy is because adoptees understand that their presenting problems reside in the past, in early trauma, yet many children referred to CAMHS or other services have no conscious recall of any trauma. They describe feeling unable to go and 'just talk about it' when they are at a loss to know what 'it' is that should be spoken. Some even describe developing a 'pseudo-narrative' of how they think they should feel, in order to relieve the demands on them to engage in therapies. Jamillia, an eight-year-old dual heritage girl stated to me, 'I had to go and see this old white guy and explain why I was being naughty…he just didn't get me…so I told him I was bad cos I missed my birth mum.'

In my own practice, I began working as a 'last resort' therapy for families who had run the gauntlet of other services, yet were still presenting in crisis, many at the point of adoption breakdown. This book aims to bring music therapy more into the forefront of the minds of those thinking about referrals because of its special capacity to work with that which is consciously unknowable and unsayable.

Music as non-verbal language

All of the creative expressive arts therapies potentially offer something different and useful for adoptive families, because of their non-verbal modality. Although we may describe specializing in working with clients around adoption-specific needs, we are very likely as music therapists to find that the adoptive families referred to us have additional and complex needs. Frequently, adopted children are referred to me who were difficult to place initially because of significant physical and learning disabilities, and who present additional challenges in adoptive placements because of these difficulties, conflated with their attachment and trauma needs. These children are often non-verbal themselves, and so need access to therapies that do not rely on spoken language. Other children will have experienced complex early trauma, prior to their possessing language. Some children will have been separated at birth from their birth mother, which itself is hugely traumatic (as Nancy Verrier describes in *The Primal Wound* 1993). Others will have been removed from their birth families because they experienced abuse from a birth parent. Their trauma cannot be spoken about because it occurred when they were at a pre-linguistic stage of development. As such, they are unable to consciously know and describe it and make sense of it cognitively. Instead, it remains deeply layered in the body and in unconscious memory. The arts therapies offer hope that this deepest of places might be accessible through mediums that work symbolically, and might access unconscious experience that happened prior to language acquisition.

Why then is music therapy an especially useful modality, when other creative arts therapies could equally be helpful for adoptive families? First, music possesses specific qualities such as rhythm, timing, intensity and dissonance, which are discussed in the literature of verbal psychotherapy, and increasingly so in the fields of relational embodied psychotherapy (Trevarthen 1979; Stern 1985; Beebe and Lachmann 2002; Tronick 2007; Totton 2015). These musical qualities are similar to those that figure in early psychological development as described by Stern (1995, 1998). Stern defines the musicality of 'proto-conversation' at the core of the relationship between mother and infant before language is established, expressing the desire to attune to one another. Almost all adoptees I work with experienced early loss of their maternal figure, and subsequently could not develop that first pre-verbal attuned relationship with their birth parent. This traumatic loss remains unconscious because it happened at a pre-verbal stage of life. Early trauma cannot be accessed through language because the experience predates language. It remains unconscious, yet alive. The co-creation of music between therapist and client has similar musical elements to the co-creation of relationship between mother and child, and can therefore offer reparation where this relating has been lost to an adopted child. A music therapy relationship has value in evoking the early situation with its use of the same musical elements that appear in proto-conversation.

Early on in my own practice with adoptees, I noticed that when clients were leading the improvisations they instinctively sought out elements of repetition and regularity in their music-making, and unconsciously gravitated naturally to utilizing forms such as ostinato. These repetitious, circling musical features can in and of themselves provide containment, self-soothing, and affect regulation (as described by Stern 1994). Structured musical elements can provide a frame for self-regulation with adopted clients wherein their losses, traumas and subsequent attachment and attunement needs can be repeated and more safely thought about. The Jungian analyst and trauma expert Margaret Wilkinson (2010) states that people who have experienced trauma require therapy that provides a modified response, and a different affective experience through relating with another at the deepest levels both consciously and unconsciously. Music therapy provides an audible shaping to emotional experience, which can both reveal and hold unconscious trauma and internalized patterns of relating, while simultaneously eliciting new affective experiences within the therapeutic relationship.

It is evident then that musical elements can provide a felt sense of containment very similar to the core aspects a baby needs in an early attachment relationship in order to experience attunement – and what adoptees so often have lacked. As music therapist Jacquie Robarts (2014) has stated, musical expression directly engages and activates the core of rhythmic and sympathetic impulses from which all human communication comes. Musical expression in and of itself is not magical, however, but rather music therapy has something special to offer because of the way musical elements are employed *in the relational space* between client and therapist. Music can become something like the 'third object' (Ogden 1992) because it is a transient temporal form. It exists as an attentional, acoustic safe 'space between' therapist and client which is fed into by both, but which also can impact on and feed back to both. Both the embodied aspect of how clients play music and their sounds and relational music-making potentially contain all the elements of attachment formation and attuned relating. Adopted children might therefore find safety in the co-creation of needs-led freely improvised music, trusting their own phrasing and patterns, while hearing a therapist playing with them. Grounded in their own music, they can thus begin to process and assimilate the emotional impact of their traumatic experience within a musical relationship. This is why the approach I have evolved is described as client-led, because only as the client is able to lead, shape and control the music that emerges is there potential for early relational patterns and needs to literally be 'played out'.

The early trauma of adoption

Knowledge of the impact of early life experience has become more mainstream during the past few years, and the growing body of work within neurobiology has given scientific credence to much that psychotherapy has been positing for decades. Adoptive parents coming to therapy now are to some extent at least aware from their months or years of lived experience with their adopted child that early experience cannot just be 'loved away'. Trauma lingers and will stretch its tentacles into the present, impacting negatively and severely on relating in the here and now. Families will probably only have had a minimal amount of attachment and trauma training prior to adoption, but inevitably will have gained some knowledge about the impact of early life experience. It is therefore not too great a leap to begin thinking together with adoptive parents about what a child's mind and body had to do in order to cope when trauma happened, and what the long-term impacts even of pre-verbal and unconscious early experiences are.

In my own practice, we always begin with a pre-therapy meeting where, together with the referrer, we begin by telling families that, in the words of Babette Rothschild (2000), 'the body remembers', or as Bessel Van der Kolk (2014) puts it 'the body keeps the score'. In other words, adoptees may not consciously be able to tell us what their experiences have been, but experience resides in embodied memory, and in the very brain structures that grew from those experiences. This is why therapies that utilize the body and do not rely on cognitive processing might be able to help access traumatic early memories that are buried unconsciously, but still exert influence. Adoptive families presenting in crisis have sometimes believed at the time of placement (especially for children who have been spared the worst excesses of physical and sexual abuse and been placed with adopters at only a few days or weeks old), that all their child needs is 'lots of love'. This is what ten-year-old Louise's adoptive parents told me they had hoped. Yet Louise smeared herself with excreta, picked wounds in herself until she bled, attacked 'anything that moved', and screamed day and night. Love was clearly not enough for this family, and Louise's parents were fortunately keen to tenderly explore the deep roots of her emotional experience.

Music therapy with adoptions in crisis

Previous music therapy work has, for the most part, been situated with new adoption placements, to help babies or very young children (already identified as having relational difficulties, described as attachment problems), to bond within their new families, and to support new adoptive parents with developing attachment styles. Work of music therapists (such as Salkeld 2008) published previously has mostly taken place at this juncture. Such preventative work, however, becomes rare when funding is scarce (such as in a political climate of austerity). Early on in my work I mostly received referrals of children who had been placed for years, and where families were living with seriously entrenched problems. Could music therapy realistically offer hope for relational changes for these children and families, or was it too late?

Adoptions in crisis ultimately result in very distressed children being faced with the scenario of returning to the care system. Both children and parents are under phenomenal stress. They, and the professionals working with them, feel hopeless. As I embarked on my own practice working with entrenched difficulty, and in the face of seeming inevitable placement breakdown, I was initially encouraged by insights emerging from neurobiology, informing current thinking on attachment and trauma. Cozolino's (2006) work confirms that the brain is not a fully formed structure, but a dynamic process undergoing constant development and reconstruction across the life span. Wilkinson (2010) likewise inspires hope undergirding working with unconscious difficulties and darkness, because of evidence of the brain's plasticity and its capacity for healing and change. An understanding of the experience-dependent plasticity of the mind-brain-body is key to the potential changing of minds and relationships in music therapy with adoptive families who present with entrenched problems.

Neuroscience has identified an emotional regulatory system, where brain cells are programmed to be activated by kind, soothing, affectionate behaviour, producing a mental state of peaceful contentment and safety. A growing body of neurobiological evidence shows that the quality of early caregiving we receive shapes and develops our neurological systems, regulating stress and enabling self-soothing. Warm, attuned caring early in life can literally turn genes off and on and influence the way brains physically develop. Throughout life though, similar caring actually continues to nourish our brains, by triggering the release of endorphins and oxytocin (chemicals produced in large quantities particularly during breast feeding, and responsible for early feelings of closeness). This is hopeful news for music therapists working with complex entrenched trauma! Carter (1998) locates the roots of human resilience in the sense of being understood by, and having the sense of existing in, the mind and heart of a loving, attuned and self-possessed other. Fosha (2003, p.29) also suggests that 'through just one relationship with an understanding other, trauma can be transformed, and its effects neutralized or counteracted'. The music therapy relationship can therefore be significant in the reparation of loss and trauma, even when this has been entrenched in life, and this is good news to share with adoptees and their families.

Supporting adoptions through relational change

How then might music therapy support adoptions and instil hope for change in families? One main objective of the rest of this book is to enable music therapists to think about their own work and how in therapeutic relationships we might best make use of the most powerful and original resource we have – our music. Also, I hope to enable other professionals to deepen an understanding of how specifically music therapy can support adoptions within the context of other post-adoption support resources.

In the next chapter, I will discuss the significance of the beginnings for adoption placements; first, how those placements are made, and how subsequent family relationships come into being, and second, how this process itself may set up relational structures with inherent problems. The remainder of this book considers what lived experiences bring adopted children, young people, and their families to music therapy post placement, and explores what music therapy can offer in terms of sense-making of diverse presentations which come under the general criteria of 'adoption difficulty'.

Adoption crisis, activating trauma in both child and adult, throws families into strange places they never dreamed of being. Parents say they no longer recognize themselves as they act out in ways that appal them. An adoptive parent described to me her extreme relationship deterioration with her daughter Suzie, stating, 'Suzie physically attacked me, but she was screaming that she knew *I* was really the one who wanted to punch *her*, and she was goading me to do so. And I did. Worse, than that, though, I felt like I wanted to annihilate her, kill her. I didn't adopt her to hate or to harm her but that's how it's become.'

Trauma and attachment issues may get lost in a whole gamut of 'signs and symptoms', which themselves may be precursors to families requesting intervention. Some adoptees accrue a specific mental health diagnosis, such as attachment disorder, attention deficit hyperactivity disorder, autism, or bipolar illness. All the children I have worked with have presented with high levels of emotional and behavioural disturbance, and a lack of progress in making meaningful relationships within their new family. Adopters often doubt their capacity to parent at all, and are self-blaming for difficulties which persistently endure many years beyond the initial placement, even in the face of their 100 per cent love and commitment. How do we as music therapists help these families to hold on to to their children and stay with them through difficult enacted experience?

When families come to music therapy, it is imperative that we recognize that there are additional supports that should be made available for them in order for the work to proceed. The music therapist's role should always form part of an extended 'team around the child'. This is especially important when working with complex multiple needs. A narrative of adoption common to all professionals in such a team can connect with diagnoses and work even in extreme child protection scenarios, with an understanding of attachment and trauma at its heart. I am fortunate to be linked with enormously experienced post-adoption teams, who possess a huge capacity for thinking therapeutically. These teams can provide additional supports to music therapy such as:

- reassurance to parents/other family members

- contact with others in similar situations to diminish shame and isolation
- reading material on attachment, trauma, neurobiology and so on
- management advice
- enhanced cognitive understanding of the child's difficulties.

The provision of conceptual frameworks can help adopters enormously, easing their sense of personal failure and enabling them to feel contained at all levels, thus delineating clear boundaries for the therapeutic role. If music therapists work in isolation we risk becoming uncontained ourselves when stresses spiral out beyond the therapy room, and when children who find it difficult to believe anyone can really safely hold them act out their fear and even bring about that very event which they fear – adoption breakdown.

Each referred family is different, presenting at a unique point in their life trajectory. My approach has always been to work in a 'needs-led' manner on a case-by-case basis, and as such I do not prescribe within this book a formal 'model for doing adoption work'. There are, however, certain common features to every case in terms of how the work is framed. Parents or social workers will consult initially about making a referral. There may then be some time spent accruing funding (most families now apply initially themselves through the Adoption Support Fund, which I discuss further in Chapter 4). Recognizing that short-term therapy could replicate the experiences and inner worlds of children well used to adults flitting in and out of their lives, I argue strongly for long-term pieces of work, necessary for sufficient containment and holding. Once funding is obtained, we proceed with an initial consultation/assessment meeting with the adopters (and child, if they are able to participate) as well as associated professionals, as deemed appropriate. These apparently simple structures of the referral process enable families to know exactly where they are in the process and can help manage anxieties spilling out before the work itself begins.

Music therapy potentially provides, in Winnicottian terms, a symbolic sense of a father holding a mother, so the mother can hold and contain the baby. As therapists, we hold the referred child who is our client, and the team assists in holding the entire family. Parents are then enabled over time to explore new ways of holding and parenting their child. Our holding happens within the space that *both* music and relationship provide. And we are held within our supervision/personal therapy.

As each individual family begins music therapy, I hold in my mind an underlying premise that is common to all adopted children: that they carry internalized knowledge of their early trauma and loss, and know in their deepest cell memory what has happened to them. This manifests in music therapy as what Margaret Wilkinson (2010, p.4) describes as 'the old present'. Children's difficult early experiences remain buried within, unknown and unknowable, but carrying an instantly recognizable feeling in the present that is often 'a meld of helplessness, rage, terror and dread' (2010, p.4). Strong emotions of distressing events, which are stored principally in the amygdala, are unavailable to conscious memory recall, yet govern ways of being and behaving.

The following example illustrates this:

CASE VIGNETTE: **JOE**

Joe, aged 11, brought contemporary pop songs to his early music therapy sessions. Superficially, there was little that was remarkable in the songs, and yet when he sang them within sessions, the quality of his voice and the earnestness with which he sang made them redolent with meaning. He repeatedly sang one verse, (one of many he potentially had access to in contemporary culture), and this repeated verse needed to be thought about differently in a therapeutic space, driven as it appeared to be by an unconscious choice. His intense, urgent, agitated singing communicated a level of emotional distress. I had initially wondered if he was using these songs as a defence and thereby avoiding entering into more exposing improvisations with me. However, in reflection within supervision it was apparent that both the lyrics and the song's musical structures were together providing an important vehicle of communication for Joe at a deep level. I therefore set up a meeting for discussion with Joe's social worker to search out any information available about his early life experience.

It transpired that the song appeared to contain an unconscious recognition of a narrative he could not consciously know he had. In fact, the verse he kept singing 'on repeat', as it were, directly described an extremely early pre-adoption experience of trauma within his birth family. Joe had refused previously to attend CAMHS, stating he could not 'talk about adoption', but it appeared that he could sing about it. Music (here in this pop song specifically shaped by musical elements such as a piano ostinato, and a circling repetitive chord sequence) seemed to provide some containment, self-soothing, and affect regulation for him where his 'old present' could be repeated and more safely thought about with a witnessing therapist. Music therapy with Joe seemed to provide that modified response described by Wilkinson. A different affective experience was occurring through relating with another at the deepest levels, both consciously and unconsciously, and all this being held at all times within the music.

The attachment communications and music of adopted children are expressed at levels beneath conscious awareness within the dynamic intersubjective field. Joe's music therapy individually with me had focused on his singing and self-accompanying. Yet, when Joe's adoptive mother, Nicola, joined us in sessions, the pop-song-playing teenager regressed, sitting instead together with her on the floor, sharing xylophones, and interacting with tiny sounds. Nicola herself identified this as 'baby Joe' needing to communicate with her, and this became perhaps a form of musical 'motherese' (Stern 1985), a language they had earlier in life been denied experiencing as he was not her birth child. When their placement was at its worst, she felt these brief moments of positive, attached behaviours sustained them. The music provided safe holding for both of them, and gave her insights into his inner world, revealed in the free space of improvising together.

Trauma response is communicated in implicit, affective, non-verbal ways. Most of the music within early sessions with adopted children has revealed chaotic internal worlds arising from early trauma, as the following example illustrates.

CASE VIGNETTE: **SHANIA**

Seven-year-old Shania lacked any spatial sense and seemed disconnected from her own body movements, yet she was a bright girl with no diagnosis of learning disability or autism. Deeply traumatised by emotional and physical abuse within her birth family, she had experienced multiple foster placements, and even one earlier adoption breakdown. Her unsurprising resultant internal chaos was expressed in embodied chaos, and even 'accidental' damage of instruments. In her first music therapy sessions, instruments would never be played but were all instead turned into weapons. Expecting me to attack her, she would rather attack me first. Yet, when she eventually began to play loud, aggressive and fractured music, her adoptive mother Annette said she could really hear 'her tears and her trauma' at last being given expression.

Transformational power may be embedded sometimes in the simplest affective interactions, and even in silence (which is of course the necessary corollary of music). The experience of silent looking and gazing at a therapist has been an important part of many adopted children's therapy. Schore (1994) demonstrates how gaze plays a crucial part in the development of a sense of self and of other and underpins all relating that develops out of the earliest relationship of mother with baby. An example of silent gazing being significant in the first stages of a music therapy is given in the following case studies.

CASE VIGNETTES: **THOMAS** AND **GEORGIA**

Eleven-year-old Thomas sat silently looking at me while I gazed back at him for a total of 11 weeks' duration before either of us ever made a sound. In later sessions, he would continue to sit holding my gaze for some minutes before he could start to play, stating once, 'If we look we might see each other.' In a similar way, nine-year-old Georgia would want me to sit close by her and share gazing with her at a drum brush. I was asked to slowly and painstakingly count every single bristle on this brush with her, before she could eventually use it to make the tiniest imperceptible sounds.

Such holding is not easy to achieve, not least because the two processes described above took a lot of time. At times, I even found myself wondering if I was being a music therapist when I was working in silence. Yet in such self-initiated and directed experiences for these clients, they could begin to experience 'being' with another as well as 'seeing and being seen by' another. Thus, they could recognize that they might exist in the mind and heart of another. In these seemingly small and silent interactions, the early ground of relational reparation was occurring. This process is continuous over the life span of an adoptee, as at particular transitions early material can become foregrounded again.

CASE VIGNETTES: **TONY** AND **NICKY**

Six year-old-Tony towards the end of his therapy created a song to sing, along with his adopters, which included the line 'Now the old king is dead! Long live the king!' Adopted children, dealing with complex situations and ideas of multiple families, need to somehow integrate both the kingdom they originated in and the new kingdom before them. Both kingdoms will endure for them.

Nicky came to music therapy at a point where her family anticipated she would return to care (and she was already in foster care respite one week a month). Nicky also focused on singing one contemporary pop song, with lyrics ostensibly describing a jilted woman wanting to find someone like her previous lover. The song for Nicky encompassed an experience of initiating contact with her birth mother (which she had done alone via an internet search, unbeknown to her adoptive parents). She was finding the consequent events unmanageable, yet was unable to allow her adopters to help. Nicky sang lyrics about feeling that she had to enter her birth mother's life 'uninvited', and that initiating contact was a way of showing her birth mother that her pain of abandonment was not 'over'. Her adoptive mother then acknowledged support of Nicky's need to search for and know her birth family, and was able to offer to help her to do this more safely, so that eventually she might be able to integrate her early and present experiences.

As adopted children create music in the presence of a witnessing therapist, relational experiences of continuity and expectation are established which might lead to shared musical participation. Bodies move together, even listening to a shared song, in synchronicity to a beat or pulse (which is perhaps not unlike 'the rhythm of safety' that Tustin described in the mother-infant relationship, 1981). Research by Gallese (2005) shows that from as early as 18 weeks' gestation, the foetus knows the intonation and timbre of the mother's voice. This is the basis of prenatal attachment through *sound*, having significance in respect to its emotional quality, relational engagement, interaction and loving affection. Trevarthen (1979) calls this 'communicative musicality' and suggests it is the base from which meaning in all relationship flows. When adopted clients therefore engage in an embodied musical relationship, their early intuitive emotional communications are able to be made evident in dynamic form. The sense of a self is then much more than just a mental construct, and becomes a tonal embodied feeling experience.

Gallese (2005) argues that such an embodied basis for empathy and intersubjectivity is essential in therapy. Music therapy happens through the body as we cannot play an instrument, or sing, without bodily engagement. The simulation and imitation of the emotional body states of others has been called 'analogic relatedness' by Knox (2011) in her description of reciprocal shaping and picturing of the emotional embodied experience of the other. As music therapists, we might more simply understand this as 'matching and mirroring'. However, embodied analogic relatedness is very different to just musically 'copying' what adopted clients play, because it is the *feelings behind* musical playing that become the referent. This is imitation, from the *inside*, of what lived experience *feels* like, not simply how it is expressed in action. Clients' emotions are constituted, experienced and therefore directly understood in embodied musical simulation, producing a shared embodied musical state. Within music therapy, we are able to sense clients' feelings in our own bodies, and they can know we empathize because of the extent we induce in our embodied music the state prevailing in theirs. Shared embodied musical expression is therefore an essential element for the emergence of intersubjectivity in music therapy with adoptees (this is discussed further in Chapter 10).

Embodied music-making and attunement possibilities

Stern's (1998) work on intersubjectivity introduces the concept of 'affect attunement'. It is this felt sense of attunement that is totally lost for children when the fundamental first relationship is totally denied to them. The impact of the loss of an adopted child's birth mother can cause serious lifelong issues. Adopted adults, removed at as young as a few days old, talk of the pain of simply being 'given up' by their birth mother, even before they ever had any problems to make them 'deserve' being given up. Infants absorb overwhelming sensations of abandonment, while not yet possessing resources for language to process and assimilate this experience. Adoptees who were babies placed in their new families at just days or weeks old become those children and adults who commonly might describe a 'hole' inside themselves. This 'hole' might function as a metaphorical description for adopted people, stemming from an attempt to describe impaired intersubjectivity, which impacts negatively on their core of rhythmic and sympathetic impulses, as well as on developing brain connectivity, self-regulation and attachment capacity. In essence, the lived experience of 'having a hole inside' stems from denied attunement. For adoption placements in crisis, a music therapy relationship might provide a creative, safe space for a sense of attunement to be re-experienced. Attunement originates in non-verbal elements of communication, and exists in the how and when of an interaction or exchange rather than its apparent content. It grows out of spontaneity, creativity and unpredictability in our work (which Stern 2004 himself beautifully calls 'sloppiness' or 'intentional fuzziness', and is described further in Chapters 3 and 7). When we work within a needs-led approach, utilizing free improvisation, both our bodies and minds are engaged in making new moments of relational experience.

As music therapists, then, we are well placed to deal with an adoptee's non-verbal unconscious material, because when we seek to attune to our clients in embodied improvisational music-making, the medium of music via its own special elements can allow both body and mind to 'speak' and to be heard. This basic rationale has underpinned the evolving psychodynamic/analytic, attachment-based, trauma-informed, embodied, relational music therapy approach I have evolved and continue to develop, and which will be described throughout the remainder of this book. The term 'model' is avoided, however, as I prefer to talk of an overarching *approach* to client-led music therapy which enables lived experience to emerge and be thought about. This leads to sense-making in new ways that can enable the emergence of new relational possibilities.

Chapter 2

The Contemporary Adoption Process in the UK

THE IMPACT OF PROCESS ON MUSIC THERAPY

It is important to state at the outset of this chapter that this book is written fundamentally from a perspective that values adoption as a permanent family formation. However, adoption is not without its problems as a means of providing permanency. It is also not the only form of permanency that is available, and may not be the right choice for every child. There is not space within the scope of this book to address other forms of contemporary permanency (such as foster care, kinship care and guardianship). Also, for children to really be able to engage in any therapy, placements need to be as stable and permanent as possible. Adoptive families are described as 'forever families' and it is this commitment to permanency, providing a secure frame for the child around music therapy, which makes working with adoptive families qualitatively different from working with other family forms. Adoption is still the only family formation where children become totally the legal children of their adoptive parents, where birth parents no longer have any legal claim to their child, and thus permanency is established in law (Bridge and Swindells 2003).

However, creating a seemingly 'happy ending' for a child, by family-forming via adoption, might equally become the starting point of pain and distress for both the child and their future adopters, unless careful consideration is given to the process. An understanding that the child's needs are paramount is essential (as is enshrined in the Children Act 2004) when they are not themselves in a position to make choices about family permanency. Professionals who act to make decisions on behalf of relinquished or looked-after children carry the weighty responsibility of removing a child from their birth family and placing them in another family for life. Most music therapists will never be part of the process of family finding and making, nor be aware of the complex decisions and legal processes that are gone through by social workers and other professionals as adoption placement decisions are made. Yet the adoption process is itself an important part of the narrative of the child and the parent/s, and will often arise within music therapy. It is important then to give some consideration to what it entails.

Modern adoption is difficult and complex. An adoptive parent cited in *The Guardian* newspaper (November 2012) summed up the risks of placement in the resultant lived experience of families, saying, 'Sometimes it brings happiness and sometimes it ruins lives.' The current and ostensibly laudable governmental idea of speedier placements for needy children risks trivializing what the adoption community and the highly trained skilled professionals who work within it have learned over decades. Children are now being placed who have experienced deep wounding and traumatic experience and are therefore likely to re-enact trauma material within their new families, who will in turn require a range of adoption support services. These services are highly contested for, having been reduced under governmental policies of austerity. Reductions are justified in a political discourse of the privatized family that can remedy its own ills and should therefore not need 'expensive' therapy.

In the 1980s, it was common in some areas for therapists working within child psychiatry to be taught that treating an adopted child was no different from treating any other child. The child was seen as the 'property' of the adoptive parents, in much the same way that all children were, by legal definition (as both parental rights and marital rights evolve from property law). There was scant attention paid to trauma that may have occurred in the child's most early experiences, and a view still persisted that what could not be consciously remembered could not be affecting a child's experience in the here and now. Even if children had later traumatic experience, the family was seen as providing its own resources to deal with this. Babies who were adopted almost from birth and certainly within weeks of being born were not really considered to have a background of trauma. It is only now (largely through the narratives of adult adoptees who have courageously written about their lived experience) that we are alive to the enduring effects of trauma, and to the particularly enduring loss of a birth mother and family (and contingent losses of society and culture). The landscape for therapeutic practice has changed dramatically within the past 30 years. Currently, there are almost daily advances being made in neurobiology which provide 'hard evidence' of trauma and its effects on the developing brain and body. Also, we now have access to incredibly creative stories by well-known people in the public domain who are able to describe the impact of being adopted as a tiny baby, and the lifelong struggles that this lived experience might result in as an adult begins a journey for themselves of sense-making.

Before addressing the difficulties that might arise in adoption, it is important to establish what we might refer to as a 'good enough' adoption for adoptees. The adoption and attachment expert Dan Hughes (1997) suggests that when adoption works well, it contains the following elements:

- A positive family atmosphere.
- Positive relationships.
- The provision of missed developmental experience (including regression).
- Thoughtful parental responses to difficult child behaviour.
- Sensitive understanding and management of a child's rage.
- An emphasis on emotional attunement.
- A capacity to provide discipline with empathy.
- A different style of parenting conducive to growing attachment.
- Overall playful, curious, accepting, empathic relating.

How then might the adoption process begin to create and inculcate placements for children with prospective adopters that might develop into 'good enough' adoptive families? Placements are initially made (after a plan from a social worker has been considered) by an adoption panel, and then ratified in a legal process that follows. Panels can be either local authority panels, or otherwise organized by an adoption charity (such as Coram, Barnardo's, Adoption UK, Adoption Matters, Adoption Focus and so on). An adoption panel is a group of mostly specialist adoption practitioners, and must be comprised of local authority and independent social workers, medical and legal advisors, and those with 'other relevant professional experience' (such as a therapist, educational psychologist). Also, panel formation guidance states that panels must include an adopted person and an adoptive parent. This is because the lived experience of both adoptees and adopters is seen as valuable professional experience.

The panel is tasked with making some of the most difficult, permanent decisions about vulnerable lives. There are in essence three main tasks of an adoption panel:

1. The approval of a social work plan for a child to be adopted.

2. The approval of a potential adopter/s.

3. The matching of a child with an adopter/s.

There is the possibility of music therapists becoming panel members, either professionally, as music therapists, or because they identify as having lived experience of adoption. So what information about lived experiences might the panel hear and have to make sense of in the process of creating placements? How might this link with the music therapist's role, first possibly as a member of a panel, and later when working with the consequences of placements that have been made?

An adoption panel considers the stories of children's circumstances that have led their social workers to consider adoption as a recommended 'permanency plan' for a child; inevitably these are stories of immense pain, sadness and loss. Children coming to adoption experience severance of the most fundamental relationship, with their birth mother, and lose most other birth relatives too, as well as losing access to their birth community, society and culture. It is imperative then that adoption is viewed as the only way forward if a family can no longer be supported to stay together. (This itself may be a more problematic decision than it first might seem, as supports that are available to vulnerable families have decreased in recent years, in accordance with an increase of admissions to the care system. Therefore, children are coming into the system earlier, with less trauma experience, but with fewer experiences of attachment.)

'Birth parent' is the term used to describe the child's parent/s in their family of origin from which they are being removed. Birth parents' stories are also painful to hear, and it is sadly not uncommon for birth parents themselves to be survivors of multiple abuses and trauma, with lived experience of the care system. Birth families are those additionally under multiple stresses from a lack of employment, or without access to extended family support, and such experiences in their adult lives, coupled with their own trauma histories, mean they are not able to make use of what little supports are available. Some birth parents may have disabilities that mean they are unable to adequately parent their own children on their own, yet these children are nonetheless loved and wanted. A few parents may have had an unexpected pregnancy (either as young people themselves who feel unable to yet provide for a child, or as mature adults who feel unable to sustain another child physically, psychologically and financially). Occasionally, a pregnancy may result from stranger rape or familial incest. It is rare in contemporary processes for a baby to be relinquished without there being a complex narrative for that baby to encounter in later life. Children are removed from complex situations where it would seem possible for anyone to make sense, cognitively, of the rationale to remove. Long term, this will of course be the task for adoptees as young adults when they might seek to trace their birth parents and learn about their early history, and try to understand why they were not able to stay with their birth family. Cognitively, it may seem obvious to an outsider that a child needed to be removed, but the emotional sense can be very different for an adoptee.

Potential adopters' stories also carry their lived experiences of the pain of their infertility, or bereavement. Adult potential parents come to adoption from varying positions. A heterosexual couple may have had numerous attempts at in-vitro fertility treatment (IVF) and be desperate for a child to call their own (a baby ideally). Others may have had children who have died, and they may not be able or even want to conceive again. Single people may have wanted to establish a permanent partnership or marry and have children, and in the event of this not happening may decide to adopt. Gay and lesbian couples may have chosen not to pursue routes such as artificial insemination or sperm donation for various reasons, and come to offer an adopted child a home. A few adopters may be able to have their own children but choose not to, for altruistic reasons. Potential adopters can, however, carry desperate narratives of desire for a child, and in their desperation can be blinded to the complex journey that adoption may turn out to be. This is why the assessment process matters and why music therapists can offer experience to panels regarding how people manage the adoption journey beyond the initial matching and placement.

Adopted children

Historically, adoption meant infant adoptions, mostly. In the 1800s, the process was one where babies described as 'illegitimate' were made available to 'good families', often via religious societies. However, it is a simplified and enduring myth that little orphaned babies needed loving parents. Rather, unmarried mothers could not afford to rear children alone, and were not supported to do so, as there was enormous societal stigma of illegitimacy.

Little thought was given in the past to potential longer-term needs of either relinquished children or their adopters, because a 'happy ever after' seemed guaranteed. An unwanted baby was placed with people who wanted a baby. Solution! Adoptees were not told of their origins as secrecy was encouraged, and only now are we aware of some of the miscarriages of justice that occurred for these children. Relinquished babies (that is, babies who are willingly given up by their birth mother rather than being removed against their will) still risk being constructed as 'easy' adoption cases. There is no history of sustained abuse or neglect to manage, and therefore adopters are seemingly given a 'clean sheet'. Adopters may come hoping to be given a baby, and assuming that this will offer the best possibility for the placement working out. Developments in attachment theory, however, show the impact of loss of the birth mother (possibly the child's most early attachment figure) causing serious issues for a child, and identity issues (among others) later in life. Discussion with adopted adults relinquished at birth reveals their confusion about their earliest moments. This can lead to them imagining that they must somehow be intrinsically bad in order for a birth parent to have let them go. Nancy Verrier (1993) describes this lived experience as an open, enduring, emotional wound. Research with adult relinquished adoptees shows the significance of identity and what it means to grow up not knowing *anything* coherent about one's self-origins, often resulting in a fundamental enduring sense of displacement, at best. Jeanette Winterson's autobiography, *Why Be Happy When You Could Be Normal?* (2011), cites her own descent into depression and suicidal behaviour, which in therapy she was able to locate back to her experience of abandonment (another possible term for 'relinquishment') as a baby.

Unmarried single parents now are far more likely to keep their babies, and it has therefore become rarer that relinquished babies are available for adoption. According to the British Association for Adoption and Fostering, only 2 per cent of children adopted during 2011 were under one year, 71 per cent were aged one to four and 24 per cent aged five to nine (British Association for Adoption and Fostering 2011). Occasionally, babies born with disability are brought to an adoption panel when birth parents themselves do not feel able to offer their child what they will need for life, or they are judged externally as being unable to provide for them. Sometimes, parents with learning difficulties themselves lose their children as a result of being deemed unable to care for them. Birth parents who have themselves experienced trauma and abuse and struggle to emotionally care for their children may contest the removal of their children and legal battles can persist for years after the adoption, causing immense stress to a placement.

Increasingly, in contemporary practice we see older children coming for adoption. Why then are such children removed by the state and presented for adoption? Children are legally removed from their birth parents and taken into care as a result of having experienced neglect or emotional, physical and/or sexual abuse. Current ideology enshrined within the Adoption and Children Act 2002 (cited in Bridge and Swindells 2003) purports that children are best looked after in their families. Recognizing the damage inherent in removal, work takes place to sustain children at home until it is impossible to do so. Removed children may then have experienced years of neglect and abuse. They might, if lucky, have experienced one good foster placement prior to adoption, but many children have multiple placements and numerous caregivers. One 14-year-old boy I worked with therapeutically had 13 placements prior to the age of three and was (unsurprisingly) described by his social worker as 'possibly having a resulting attachment disorder'. When he was finally taken to his adoptive family home aged three, he reportedly sat still on the floor and did not engage with anyone in the room in any way. It was as if he had given up on even trying to attach to people.

The various solutions other than adoption mentioned earlier might be attempted to achieve long-term security and future adult wellbeing for older children, yet following breakdown of these options, an adoption plan may be recommended for a child as old as seven, occasionally even older. Sometimes, plans are made for sibling groups to be placed together, or for the sad separation of larger groups, perhaps of five or more children (or, in one case that I was part of the decision-making panel for, the separation of 11 siblings). These are difficult children to place, with traumatic experiences, difficult relational and attachment histories, and incredibly complex narratives. Research by McCann and colleagues (1996) and Dimigen and colleagues (1999) shows that such looked-after children have more mental health difficulties and a much higher incidence of disruptive behaviour than other children and will carry these difficulties into their new adoptive families. *It matters* who is placed where, and the adoption panel must think carefully both about the best plans for children already in care, and the lifelong implications for those who would parent them. Thinking and planning take time and care if we are to get it 'right'.

Adoptive parents

A journey into parenting by adoption also has diverse routes. Potential hopeful adopters are married or unmarried, heterosexual/gay/lesbian couples, single people, gay, straight, of varying ages and from diverse cultural groups, offering a variety of permanency options.

Adopters bearing the pain and disappointment of infertility and failed fertility treatment offer a potential but painfully empty space for a child to move into. Adopters who have experienced the death of their own birth child offer a space holding memories of an absent child, and immense loss. Adopters who come already with birth children but sensing 'incompleteness' in their family size, and desiring more children, or possessing an altruistic desire to provide a home for a child who needs one, offer a space where other children are already present. (Statistically, the highest risk of placement breakdown is within families where a birth child already lives, who may be perceived as an overwhelming threat as a sibling to an adopted child.) Some adopters choose not to have a birth child (though there is no reason they could not or have not done so) and wish to become a family by the process of adoption.

For the adoption panel, potential adopters need to somehow show they have 'dealt with' their losses and pains significantly enough to manage taking on a traumatized child. Yet, what does it actually mean to have 'dealt with' infertility or the other huge losses cited above? By imagining that such lived experiences may be once and for all somehow 'resolved', there is a danger that issues arising later from pre-adoption experiences will not be thought about, or, worse, that adopters will feel blamed if they have further struggles in these areas – struggles that are very likely going to be rekindled by their adoptive children.

Social services have been criticized by the government for the lengthy home study that adopters experience prior to approval, and the perceived delaying of placements. This time and space provides potential adopters with an opportunity to examine their own internal world and think of their own attachment history and expectations of parenting. Without such work, and the insights gained, it is likely that people coming to adopt will parent as they were parented (given that this is most people's template for parenting style). Often adopters say at the adoption panel that their own need for a child drove them to adopt, but that the home study and additional training in attachment helped them recognize the complex needs of children removed for adoption, and equipped them, at least initially and partially, to re-parent an older traumatized child.

The work of Fahlberg (1994), Hughes (1997) and Howe and Fearnley (1999) shows that traditional culturally described 'parenting skills' need adapting if adopters are going to meet the needs of children with profound attachment difficulties consistent with their histories of abuse and trauma.

Children coming for placements are no longer in need of 'love' in an ordinary family sense; in fact, that may be the last thing they can cope with. Kate Cairnes (2002), an author for the British Association for Adoption and Fostering, and herself an adoptive parent and psychotherapist, describes the notion of 'therapeutic parenting' – a very different way of managing adopted children. Potential adopters now routinely attend attachment training (although this can be woefully brief, such as three days), because if they as adoptive parents do not grasp the need for therapeutic parenting, or feel that what worked for a birth child will work for an adopted child, there is a higher risk of breakdown.

Adoption placements and later life outcomes

Adoption is then both complex and rich because the multiple narratives that lead to placement involve multiple losses interacting in all manner of ways during the outworking of family life over the following years. An adoption panel places children hopefully, but rarely sees longer-term consequences of decisions made. As music therapists, we do hear the ongoing stories. We also hear how (if adoptive families are not supported with services shaped by an understanding of trauma and attachment and how these work out relationally) early life experiences of loss and abuse are re-enacted, resulting in family crisis and even adoption breakdown.

In 2012, Michael Gove (himself an adoptee) put forward the opinion that children in care looking for adoptive families needed love, and that this was adequate to ensure placement success (Gove,

2012). This view was made evident in subsequent government policy and still continues to permeate it. Yet Bettelheim's text written as early as 1950 entitled *Love Is Not Enough* articulated that much more was required. Time and again this is borne out in practice. There is a risk that at the interface of placement, trauma meets trauma, as adults have all their own loss 'buttons' pressed by children who behave in ways that bewilder, frustrate and ultimately repel and wear down their adopters. The adopted child's behaviour is a search for understanding from their adopting adults, yet adopters may become unable to do anything but arch away in the opposite direction.

CASE VIGNETTE: **MADDIE**

Maddie was 17, nearly 18. Beginning to search for her birth family, she obtained a report detailing her birth parents' drug misuse and child abuse, culminating in the eventual suicide of her birth father. However, Maddie stated that she hated social workers for removing her as a baby from her parents and thus 'denying' her a relationship with her birth father. Maddie was herself using drugs and behaving extremely chaotically, placing herself in danger of re-enacting the script she had been given. *Yet,* she was removed at just six weeks old, with no conscious memory of the extreme neglect from her mother (who was using heroin at the time), which necessitated this removal. She was unable to consider at all that a decision to remove her had been made in her best interests when she was at risk. She had been deeply loved by her adoptive parents since her placement with them as a tiny baby, yet resented them and said she would have preferred to have been left where she was.

CASE VIGNETTE: **CARRIE**

Carrie was referred for 'extreme behaviour problems' including an unplanned pregnancy resulting in termination. In assessment, her adoptive mother, struggling to cope, stated through her tears, 'When I see her promiscuity, and how easily she conceived a child, all I remember is my inability to do this thing, and I'm so jealous.' Carrie also had been adopted at six weeks old, and was very loved, yet she taunted her adoptive mother regarding her fertility, telling her she had been 'too ugly' to have a baby.

Adoption placements in crisis

What might be going on, then, with adoption placements in crisis, and how might our sense-making that we do together with the families influence and shape the music therapy we provide?

Children (who are acting out trauma in adoptive families) can carry the blame for placement failings (rather than the trauma itself) and generate referrals to music therapy because of the pathology they tend to accrue. They often know that they are pathologized, blamed and seen as needing to be 'helped' or 'fixed'. Children describe verbally (if they are able) feeling a desperate, weighty responsibility because of experiences they cannot help but enact in placement. Such emotional sensations may present early on in the music.

CASE VIGNETTE: ALICE

Seven-year-old Alice, adopted with her three male siblings, was painfully monitoring their behaviour, becoming overly 'good' herself and controlling of their boisterousness. She was living in desperate fear that this placement, their second adoptive placement, would break down. The siblings' first adoptive placement had failed after just two weeks, as the adoptive parents (seemingly well prepared) said they simply could not cope with the boys' behaviour. Alice believed they had all been rejected because of her brothers' 'naughtiness' and therefore she was desperately trying to restrain her siblings and also contain any of her own impulses that she felt might be construed as 'naughty'. Her playing in our early musical sessions was always extremely careful and quiet, and the instruments were handled delicately. She always asked what her therapist wanted to play and presented a false self in her desperation to keep everything good.

Children will present differently in music therapy, depending on their internal working models derived from their early care experience and how their internal world beliefs are being played out in their adoptive placement. Bowlby (1998) described how infants construct these internal working models based on experiences with their earliest attachment figures. Beliefs about the self, others and relationships provide templates setting boundaries and determining how relationships with other people are perceived and managed. Children who experience multiple placements prior to adoption vary hugely in their perceptions of the intentions and motives of others. Parental love is not enough to help these children develop necessary emotional regulation and reflective function. Traumatic experience that was prolonged, multi-layered and experienced at the hands of a caregiver results in the accumulation of negative persecutory patterns in children's minds, predicting the likelihood of dire future experiences of relating. Within music therapy, we may well find ourselves dealing with the complex inner worlds of children, peopled with numerous negative figures.

Adopters will themselves have internal working models which influence their parenting. Delaney (1998) describes a pattern of cyclical relationships between a child and their adopter, which offers a theory for how adoption placements can end up in difficulty. The continuing behaviours of children with a history of abuse and trauma almost inevitably confuse and bewilder their adopters (however well prepared and trained), who then begin to feel their parenting strategies are ineffective, leading them to doubt their own abilities as carers and adoptive parents. Systematic undermining of adopters' confidence and ability can lead them to emotionally or literally reject their child, thus confirming the child's internal working models (and possibly validating their own internal idea that they should somehow never be parents as they just aren't 'good at it'). Unthinking or unaware professionals risk blaming (albeit obliquely) such parents for failing their children if this relational dance is not understood and acknowledged. Alternatively, adoptive children can be blamed and described as 'too difficult for any adoptive placement'. In addition, adopters may be overwhelmingly painfully reminded of their pre-adoption infertility, or report renewed grieving for a dead child when experiences with their adopted children do not correspond to residual fantasy images of a lost birth child.

The 'problem' of adoptions ending up in crisis then is located in the interface of the relationship between child and adult where trauma interacts with trauma and presents in the following ways:

- Disillusionment and despair about the placement (for all parties).
- Self-doubt and self-blame (in both children and parents).
- Feeling deceived about the lived reality of placement (parents).
- Feeling emotionally overwhelmed by the child's enduring needs (parents).
- Experiencing a painful lack of a reciprocal attachment from their child, possibly accompanied by the child's loyalty to their birth family, even those who have perpetrated horrendous abuse on them (parents).

This is a huge emotional burden for adoptive parents who constantly receive their children's enacted pain. When such parents finally arrive in music therapy they often report feeling blamed and judged by professionals, and also might report earlier negative experiences of therapy where specific problems associated with adoption, trauma and attachment may not have not been thought about.

There is an additional problem with regard to accessing music therapy that when a child is adopted, most funding dries up because adoptive parents become full legal parents. Care is the 'responsibility' of adoptive parents, and no longer the state. Inevitably, this means that blame for failure must be posited somewhere – often with the adoptive parents. Frustrated workers may unconsciously hold internal beliefs that families 'got what they wanted', so what are they complaining about? The introduction of the Adoption Support Fund has done much to mitigate this issue and made funding more accessible, but perhaps even more significantly has opened up a discourse about adoption that incorporates the idea of lifelong access to supports being necessary.

Contemporary adoptive families are dealing with complexities simply unheard of years ago. Relinquished babies historically had no contact with birth families, and often grew up without even knowing they were adopted. Now contact is almost routine in some form or another, sometimes via 'Letterbox' (a system where birth parents and adoptive parents exchange written information annually, including photographs), or sometimes actual face-to-face contact with a parent, sibling, or grandparent, in an open-adoption context. Adopters manage a whole different set of dynamics if their child has yearly contact with 'real' family members. Contact can be perceived even as re-traumatizing, and stressful for all to manage. By the time children and families are referred for music therapy, the situation can feel hopeless. It is important to recognize this with families, and even to hear talk of placements ending if we are to truly engage with the reality of lived experience.

Adoptive families shoulder a burden of care, and are hoping to 'mend damage' in their children on behalf of society. Adopted children who find a sense of home and stability are much less likely to act out distress later in life, or to re-enter the care or criminal justice systems. Surely, therefore, society has a duty of care towards adopters and a moral imperative to support and resource adoption, rather than insist that families heal by their own loving? Adoption status is lifelong, yet, ironically, all support from children's services, until very recently, ended on the child's 18th birthday (the very time that an adopted child has the independent right to seek out their birth family). The adoption community articulates a desire to be able to have lifelong access to specialist supportive resources, not necessarily continual therapy, but an accessible, flexible, enduring system, because being adopted is a lifelong experience. Children's services have, over time, become sensitized to adoption work, but adult services are less aware and less responsive to the needs of adult adoptees (especially if there is competition for resources from other groups). Legislative change is required to ensure the full extent of children's difficulties can be acknowledged so that appropriate support might be routinely offered. Otherwise, as families learn to their cost post placement, the government call for faster universal adoption is unwise. A lifelong process needs enough space and time to be worked with. In Chapter 4, I describe in more detail the development of the Adoption Support Fund, which supplies funding for families nationally and equitably to access therapy for adopted children.

As music therapists, we are part of the specialist supportive resources that adoptive families may seek to access. It is important that as we consider working in adoption we become fully apprised of the various difficulties families will have encountered throughout their journey to adopt and beyond. Only then will we be able to offer the sort of music therapy the adoption community requests – a therapy without blame or judgement that can truly engage with the complex lived experiences of adopters and adoptees.

Chapter 3

Sense-Making of Lived Experience

A THEORETICAL APPROACH

Having ascertained in the opening chapters that the adoption community believes music therapy has something to offer to its members, and having described the sorts of difficulties individuals and families are likely to present with, I will now describe how my own approach to working in a needs-led way has evolved, and what my own sense-making process has entailed. My music therapy practice in adoption has its genesis and evolution directly in the experiences I encounter with adoptees and their families in the music therapy room, while being undergirded by core theoretical concepts which I continue to add to. The broad theoretical stance that informs my practice incorporates many elements which are drawn on as seems relevant and helpful to what the client presents. It is not possible within the confines of a single chapter to describe all contributing theory in depth so this chapter will focus on key concepts, illustrated with case material.

Fundamental to my approach is an in-depth knowledge of *attachment theory*. There is not scope within this book to discuss the history and development of attachment theory, and so at the end of this chapter further reading resources are suggested. Also, many trainings now exist solely in attachment which music therapists might consider taking to boost their knowledge from that acquired in music therapy training. A limited list of these is also provided.

In essence, Bowlby started to develop attachment theory after World War Two, with his early ideas formulated in a report for the World Health Organization. By 1953, Bowlby had categorized the types of reactions children demonstrated when separated from their caregivers which indicated their attachment style (Bowlby 1953). He further developed his thinking with Mary Ainsworth (1978), whose own research on mother-infant separations resulted in the 'strange situation' procedure which was designed to assess the type of attachments infants had specifically with their mothers. Much contemporary research has also devised tools for assessing specifically father-infant attachments. In adoption panel work, the quality of sibling attachments is also thought about, especially if decisions are being made to separate sibling groups. Music therapists, therefore, need to be fully appraised of attachment theory and its contemporary developments in order to approach adoption work and share theoretical and philosophical understandings with other specialist professionals. This is because early experience of attachment relationships is assumed to be a decisive factor for the way children both create bonds and also see themselves in relation to the outside world.

Equally fundamental to my approach is the broad thinking of *classical psychoanalysis*, especially about the earliest relationships in life and why these matter, because these ideas are pertinent to work where the loss of the earliest relationship is at the heart of the problems. The British psychoanalytic school of thought helps us to understand the impact and enduring effects of the loss of early attachment figures, both when the briefest early attachment relationships with a birth family are severed through adoption, or when children's attachments are impacted by trauma (emotional, physical or sexual abuse) prior to adoption.

Additionally, my approach incorporates *developmental theorists* (including, but certainly not limited to, Stern, Trevarthen and Winnicott), *relational psychoanalytic theorists* (such as Knox and Wilkinson), *neurobiology theorists* (such as Schore), *neuroaffective theorists* (such as Bentzen and Hart), *embodiment theorists* (such as Rothschild, Van der Kolk and Totton), *trauma theorists* (such as Bateman, Fonagy and Siegel), and *trauma and disability theorists* (such as Corbett, Cottis and Sinasson). The work of these theorists is discussed throughout the remainder of this book.

Over a period of years, I have found that my approach is turning to focus more deeply on the core concepts of Bion, Stern and Winnicott, which are most often in my thinking and discussions as I engage in sense-making with families and professionals about the lived experience of adoptees in music therapy. The remainder of this chapter considers how specific theories of theirs have become central to my approach.

Stern

Daniel Stern's (1998) work on attunement is core reading on almost every music therapy training course in the UK, such is the perceived relevance of his ideas in contributing to how we explain a music therapy relationship. My own PhD research focuses on what I have termed 'micro-moments of attunement', and the significance of these in the renewal and repair of relationship styles in adoptive families. Stern never discussed any of the arts therapies in his writings, and he never worked (at least as far I am aware) with a music therapist. His ideas, however, focused as they are on non-verbal moments of relating in early life and the enduring significance of these, are applicable to the adoption client group. This group are often working with material that originated from the pre-verbal time of their lives, or indeed are continuing to reside in a non-verbal world due to disability. His ideas are also relevant to our non-verbal modality of music.

Stern's (1977, 1995) studies began with his observations and video analysis of mother-infant relationships, which he explored in microscopic detail. He suggested that the unfolding of this 'first relationship' between mother and infant is mirrored in the later unfolding of relational interactions between two people, and thus can be helpful in understanding the interactions happening between a therapist and client. We find our beginnings in the first relationship, and often repeat these later in life, for good or bad.

Stern (2004) later adapted his microanalytical style to deeply explore the moment-to-moment interactions occurring in psychodynamic therapy sessions. He developed a terminology for different moments within the 'flow' of the session which he defined as 'moving along', 'now moments' and 'moments of meeting'. I initially hypothesized that what I was also observing and studying in close analysis and video of music therapy sessions was nearest to his defined 'moments of meeting'; however, my own microanalysis to date of music therapy sessions with adoptees leads me to consider that 'moving along' more closely describes what I and my clients are experiencing and engaging with in our sense-making.

Stern (2004) and 'moving along'

Stern suggests that 'moving along' is a state in which a mother and infant play together, enjoying one another just for the sake of it. There is no specific end goal in their play, which does not function as a means to an end, but rather the two are enjoying being with one another and improvising their relating together. Stern suggests it is the *improvisatory* nature of moving along which allows implicit relational knowing (which is largely non-verbal) to surface. As this moving along is open to allowing for the unexpected, it means this enjoyable relationship is open to the possibility that other pivotal 'moments' might emerge. Stern goes on to make it implicit that 'change' (whatever we consider that might be) can occur without sudden dramatic moments, and actually occurs during the quieter, less charged moments of relating. The experience of 'moving along' is subtle and needs repetition in order for change to occur.

As I read these descriptions, I recognize a process that seems similar to what I so often both feel and know and experience in my relationships with clients in the therapy room, and is also resonant with what clients themselves report experiencing.

There is never any 'end goal' that I aim towards in adoption music therapy. The work resists any attempt to be reduced to aims, goals or outcome measures. Instead, a space is offered wherein the client and music therapist can meet and begin a relationship. As the music therapist endeavours to allow whatever happens to happen, so the music therapist and client can begin to shape understandings of what is happening both musically and relationally. Initially, this will give insights into unconscious patterns of relating, stemming from early experience, and later in the work it is hoped that the music therapy relationship will offer a place for experimentation with new styles of relating. Stern's concept of moving along helped me to give attention to what is described later in Chapter 9 as offering 'presence' and 'simply being' in the music with a client, as this fundamental aspect of the ground for relating can itself effect significant change in the 'implicit relational field'. Analysis of video of my own sessions at a micro-level showed that indeed it was those less charged moments of musical relating that seemed to lead to changes in the client's relational style (this was often confirmed to me by feedback from parents, and older verbal children). Such moments, however, cannot be reduced to techniques which might be performed in the same way with different clients to gain the same effects every time (the gold standard of being replicable that much research aims for) because of the very fact that they are relational moments. When we engage in a free client-led improvisation, we cannot know how the music may develop, and we do not know how it will end. We just begin to play together, and thereby to musically relate together, and it is in the playing that relational dynamics emerge.

This idea of 'moving along' feels redolent of ideas of Winnicott's which similarly undergird my work. Winnicottian theories have perhaps been more influential on the stance of adoption practice I have evolved for myself than any others. From Stern's mother-infant observations it is apparent that as much as the baby needs the mother to 'do' things, it is equally important that she stops 'doing' to the baby in order to 'be' with the baby. This state of 'being with' that a mother can enter is what Winnicott (1960) defines as 'going on being'.

Winnicott 'on going on being'

We know now from contemporary neuroscience that a baby can initiate interaction, primarily with its mother/caregiver, from the earliest of days. This is a subtle but major development in theory that previously supposed that tiny babies were not initiators, just responders. The baby therefore needs the mother to be close enough and aware enough to meet the baby's interactions and communications in a way that is neither 'abandoning' nor 'interfering'. In other words, the baby needs to not be overly managed nor overly neglected. The absolute extremes of 'interference' are the sort of intrusions that are experienced on every level when a baby/child is exposed to trauma, especially if that trauma constitutes emotional, physical or sexual abuse. Babies also can experience a different sort of interference when a mother cannot leave them alone psychologically, or cannot let them 'be' without inflicting her own needs, intrusive aims or fears. In Winnicott's (1971, p.89; emphasis added) own words:

> The mother gazes at the baby in her arms and the baby gazes at his mother's face and finds himself therein, *provided that the mother is really looking at the unique, small, helpless being and not projecting her own expectations, fears, and plans for the child.*

At the other end of the continuum, away from interference, is abandonment. The feeling sense a baby can experience when there is no authentic relating coming back to them from the mother/caregiver can create a felt sense of abandonment, even though that person is physically present. At whatever point a baby is removed from their birth mother, they will experience a loss of that potential fundamental attachment and will experience abandonment (even if the mother is against her child being removed). People who have been adopted as tiny babies often describe this felt sense of abandonment and how they have needed to erect defences against connecting and relating to avoid being abandoned again. Early lived experience plays out in this way, impacting on the adoptee's journey into adulthood, if it is not able to be expressed.

An ideal state of relational being is to be constantly in flux, moving between polarities of interference and abandonment. It will have to include a degree of necessary interference at times (such as when a baby might need protecting from something), and an equally necessary degree of abandonment (when the baby needs to be able to experience something for themselves), but no excess of either. There is a flow state in relationships over time which enables a caregiver to move along the continuum, constantly forwards and backwards, without getting stuck at either polarity. The mother therefore needs to find a sense of balance within herself, so she can offer a non-demanding presence that allows the baby to simply be. Then the baby is enabled to develop their own sense of being and self before any need to 'do' anything is required to earn maternal attention. This is how a baby learns to enjoy its own existence in the world, and is the basis of future relating.

Winnicott (1971, p.34) says that this state of relational flow or 'going on being' is the first important capacity for existing as a self:

> The mother's non-demanding presence makes the experience of formlessness and comfortable solitude possible and this capacity becomes a central feature in the development of a stable and personal self. This makes it possible for the infant to experience a state of 'going on being' out of which spontaneous gestures emerge.

Later, Winnicott describes the capacity of the developing baby/child who learns to play 'in the presence of the mother', and by this he means the child is given enough space to explore and discover the world for themselves without the mother constantly either having to reveal it to them, or push it 'in their face' as it were, nor abandoning them to discover the world unsafely. He beautifully observes a baby freely enjoying its sense of aliveness, rolling on the floor without yet possessing a full awareness of its own body parts. At some point in that baby's development, she will 'discover the thumb'. By this Winnicott means the baby will realize that her thumb is a part of herself and will draw the thumb close, first to look at it, and in time eventually drawing it into her own mouth. A mother who feels compelled to take the baby's thumb and present it to her baby, perhaps even putting it in the baby's mouth for her, will not have allowed that process of self-exploration and discovery, and is 'interfering' with the timing of the baby finding it herself. Conversely, the mother who is disinterested in her baby's discovery and development is 'abandoning' her to work everything out for herself. Either style of relating is out of balance and will have relational consequences for the future.

I frequently have this image of the baby 'discovering the thumb' in my mind when I am playing music with an adopted child. I seek to play neither too little nor too much, moment to moment, in the emerging musical relationship, trying to attune to the child's feeling states rather than imposing something of my own. The adopted child, who in their music therapy is enabled to sense that it is okay to play 'in the presence' of a 'music mother' when that presence offers safe holding and containing and manages to be non-directive, has possibilities open for exploration. Ideally, Winnicott says the end of treatment is when a child can play alone, because they have internalized that holding and containment for themselves. His definition of 'alone' though is *'being alone in the presence of another'*. It is not seen in the defensive solitary musical playing of children who are too afraid to risk relationship, but rather in the child who can creatively explore musical options in the music therapist's presence (for example, picking out a simple melody of their making while the music therapist holds a single drone). Of course, Winnicott as well as Stern was not referring to musical play, but his descriptions certainly echo what I experience as a music therapist. Such experience also feels musically as if I am engaged in the 'moving along' Stern writes of. Although the theories have subtle differences, it is possible when watching video of sessions that are a live practice of co-creating improvisational music to later describe theoretically what is happening musically in either Stern's or Winnicott's terms.

In Chapter 1, we learned that Stern, when talking about the improvisatory nature of mother-infant relationships, suggests that in therapy it might correspond to a quality he calls 'sloppiness'! This term contrasts beautifully with the certainty implied in the language of goals, objectives and standardized approaches which often impact us as music therapists. It perhaps even provides a rationale about why we need to be less certain about what *we think* our clients need, and more open to engaging in a *relationship whereby both client and therapist together gradually are sense-making about the experience.* Non-directive, client-led, improvised shared music-making can seem 'sloppy' indeed from the outside! The music itself can sound fragmented and incoherent (especially during the earlier stages of a session such as those described in Chapters 6 and 8, when a child might be needing to show and enact their trauma experience). Staff in the schools or centres where we work may sometimes wonder what on earth has happened, when the door is opened after a loud and dissonant session to reveal a room full of instruments that have been thrown and bashed and even broken. Yet, in this chaos, this sloppy non-directed place, an adopted child has space to reveal themselves and their internal worlds as they are. As music therapists, we need to offer something in our music that can first witness, then hold and contain the chaos, in order to create a state of 'being' wherein the child can safely risk revelation of material that is traumatic in nature, and which refuses to be presented tidily or neatly. As we offer such 'presence' musically, and in the ways we present ourselves as non-directive (without being abandoning), we relate together simply for the sake of relating (as Stern 1977, 1995 suggested a mother and baby ideally do). Freed from any goal or demand, we can find one another as we are, in a potential space for relating. Only then might we create possible experiences of micro-moments of attunement which powerfully impact on our implicit relational knowing of the other.

This style of therapeutic relating is not didactic, and does not necessitate the therapist identifying as the 'expert' in the room with the client being therefore a 'novice' (especially when the matter of the work is the client's own life, in which the client may well be considered more expert!). Models of therapy that do not account for the power issues that inevitably exist between the paid professional and the referred client risk losing sight of whose work this actually is. The theoretical approach and therapeutic stance I have evolved does not consider therapy as a prescribed process with a pre-determined end, as how could it possibly be so if we are truly working in a way that is non-didactic, non-directive and led by the client's needs? As music therapists, we are constantly engaging with what is ultimately the imponderable mystery of being human which resists any description that is reductionist and linear. The richness and depth of the human psyche contains some aspects which can be defined and described, and others which defy description – and the same might be said of music! Therefore, as music therapists in adoption, we need to create places of working wherein we can be content in enabling experiences for clients to 'play alone in the presence of another' without needing to look over their shoulder for validation from us.

Forms of working that are rigid and taut or that imply certainty about what needs to happen can be very unhelpful for adopted clients when the difficulties they bring from lived experience are rarely anything like so certain or understood. Clients may themselves be setting out on their journey to discover information about their origins, which may result in meeting their birth families, and nothing of that process is certain or guarantees a fairytale conclusion. Music therapy that can tolerate uncertainty is more likely to prove accessible throughout the lifelong adoption narrative. We can create spaces for being, wherein clients do not have to achieve improvements and where body and mind can simply be watched by the therapist without the need to hold on to anything or push anything away. This experience itself (regardless of what is actually going on musically) has the capacity for relational change as it provides an antidote to hurts caused by a lack of parental ability to provide interior space or make presence available. Sitting quietly present with your own experience, alongside a witnessing music therapist, without them trying to fix it for you but being able to draw alongside you and contain that experience, is reported to be deeply reparative and restorative by people who have experienced it. 'If only we can wait, the patient arrives at understanding creatively and with immense joy… The principle is that it is the patient and only the patient who has the answers' Winnicott (1969, p.711). It seems Winnicott was valuing a needs-led approach with lived experience too!

CASE VIGNETTE: **JODIE**

Jodie, now aged nine, had experienced extreme trauma at the hands of her birth mother's boyfriend who had physically and sexually abused her in her first weeks of life. Jodie was described as 'holding herself tightly together' by both her social worker and her single female parent adopter. Her adopter described that if ever she felt she was getting emotionally close to Jodie, then Jodie would 'disappear'. She would seem to enter an inner space and her eyes would glaze over and it was as if somehow a curtain had dropped down between them. Together, the social worker, adopter and I engaged in sense-making and evolved a hypothesis that Jodie needed to escape to a safe internal place because as a tiny baby this had been what she did to survive. As a baby, Jodie had been unable to run from the man who abused her and would have experienced the most extreme psychological sense of interference, in addition to the obvious physical interference.

Jodie liked listening to music alone, and said she could somehow 'lose herself' in music. Her adopted mother felt music therapy might offer her a safe space for feeling things, but with a therapist present, so she was not using music to 'lose' herself or cut off from relating. In the early days of our work, Jodie would seek to shut me out in similar ways. She would come willingly to the room, but although she was bodily present, it felt to me that she was somewhere far away in her mind and emotions. She was clearly terrified of anyone getting close to her physically, and it was important within the room to ensure that she felt as though she had space. (People who have experienced such trauma need to know in a very literal sense that they can get out of the room and away from the therapist if they feel too threatened.) Jodie would sit on a chair close to the door, which she could run out of if she needed to, without passing me. She chose to play a xylophone which was lying on a small table. Even the instrument needed to be kept at a safe distance and Jodie would pick up a beater and lean over the xylophone (the beater itself making contact, with the xylophone one step removed again). I sat on the floor on the opposite side of the room (thus giving Jodie an increased sense of her greater height and power in our shared embodiment). I used a very soft cotton wool type beater on a single large wooden bass bar. Jodie would hum to herself and rock backwards and forwards. Both humming and rocking seemed to provide self-soothing, but also created a world around her that I could not enter. For some time, I did nothing other than rock, sharing only her embodied state, almost imperceptibly. In my own body, I was giving Jodie the gentlest and almost unobtrusive sense of somebody sharing her embodied presentation. Gradually, I reached out with the beater to the bass bar and softly played once for every fourth rock back and forwards. The soft sound of the bass bar also permeated Jodie's sound world, and it existed in the sound space between us. Gradually, she stretched out an arm, leaned to her xylophone and added in the other three beats of every four. She chose not to join my beat, and it felt as if we were maintaining our separate spaces, but at the same time, the overall rhythmic pattern contained both of us. She began to vocalize short phrases with words I could not catch as they were so quiet, so I joined vocally too, sustaining a gentle hum underneath all the sounds we were making.

The work persisted in exactly this form for many weeks. It felt extremely necessary for Jodie that I didn't 'push' her any further, but that she was able to keep playing in this way, tolerating my presence while knowing she would not be invaded in the safe feeling world she had created. It may have been tempting to 'move her on' but it was essential that she was the one to initiate any developments. For the time being she was playing and I was simply present, in body and in sound, to her. She was able to exist, in the presence of another.

Winnicott (1960) states that the end result of trauma to a young psyche results in the development of a 'false self', and a compulsive cycle of 'doing' to conceal the absence of 'being'. In other words, a child learns how to push too hard, or conversely not do enough. We might notice this in ourselves in the transference arising in the relationship at times, as in the above example of Jodie, when we feel compelled inwardly to do more, or do it better, or even do it 'perfectly'. Conversely, we might be engaged musically to some extent, and playing, but feel disengaged from the emotional and felt sense of what is happening. If we get caught in such countertransference, then we risk feeling anything that 'goes wrong' in music therapy is our responsibility, and a lot of energy will get used up in this judgement. Or, we risk blaming the client for not being able to progress, and may accuse them of being stuck. This is the importance of having our own supervision and therapy relationships wherein we might experience for ourselves an emotional constancy which is predictable and reliable. When we ourselves are not invaded, nor abandoned, we can come to rely on our supports as resources that can be reached as and when needed. Music therapists need enough freedom to play authentically ourselves, while also being certain of a supportive, containing presence for our work as we face difficult moments and tease out transference and countertransference with clients.

Holding, containing, and attunement: similarities and differences

In training for music therapists, the concepts of holding and containing are core, and a risk for new therapists is losing touch with the quite differing meanings of these terms. They can become general descriptors for how we provide the setting for therapy, and there might even be a tendency to use them together as a generic description of anything we are doing. They are, however, clearly differentiated, certainly with respect to the meanings their writers intended. Holding and containing are two concepts and two distinct aspects of the facilitating music therapy therapeutic environment.

In essence, within the type of work within adoption that I have been describing, I work with a definition of 'containing' as being a quality that belongs to the therapist, whereas holding is an activity that happens in the space between therapist and client. Within a music therapy relationship, the adoptee presents material which feels often to me very much like what Bion (1962/1984) describes with regard to 'alpha' communications. This is material that the music therapist needs to contain for the client in order to make it safe and bearable. The music therapist herself takes in these alpha elements as well as containing her own feelings (especially if the therapist also has lived experience of adoption), and then presents them back to the client but in a digested form which the client can then process for themselves. Bion emphasizes that the mother must initially be receptive to her baby's feelings, but then think about them, understand them, give expression to them, and ultimately transform them. Containing in adoption work often feels like a one-person process for the music therapist in the session, who herself is contained beyond the session. Winnicottian holding seems to me to be a different thing altogether, a more relational-musical process.

Holding appears to be what I do as a music therapist in the

adoption context with all that Bion calls 'alpha-communication' material, but also with the musical material and its acoustic expression of relational feeling. Holding happens in this work, I suggest, less 'inside' the therapist and more in the intersubjective space between therapist and client. The holding, for example, of a loud sound, will be literally within the acoustic space between the client and myself as well as in each of our own ear drums. Music (and the affect expressed in or underlying the music) is held within the body, because of the nature of its acoustic expression, but the instruments and the temporal space our sessions happen in will also be holding sounds. The sounds have been made by bodies that have acted on instruments, and therefore the instruments hold both the sound and also the emotion contained within that sound. The client can therefore feel that something in addition to just the music therapist can hold their material. If we think of the music as a 'third object' (Ogden 1992, discussed in Chapter 1) then it can exist as separate from both client and therapist. This can be especially important for adoptees who may be very frightened of what might emerge that is not yet known about. They can risk musical expression of as yet unconscious material and not fear overwhelming the therapist, because the music and the instruments are sharing the holding of such material.

'Holding' describes an incredibly subtle process occurring between mother and infant that originates not just in the mother's physical holding of her baby but also her capacity to stay emotionally with the baby's raw feeling experiences. To feel psychologically 'held', babies need to have their care carefully regulated by the mother, literally through her physical care but also through her mental communications (Wright 2009). If a mother cannot adapt to her baby (or, in the case of adoption, the baby loses the possibility of his mother being able to do so), then Winnicott (1965/1990 says the baby's capacity for creative action will be diminished or impaired.

For Winnicott (1960), repeated reliable experiences of a loving, mutually holding 'mirror' gaze between mother and infant are the remedy against negative patterns arising in a baby's internal world. Such gaze prevents hopelessness arising. The mother's face is likened to an emotional 'mirror' which the baby looks into. As he sees the mother's responses to him through her facial expression, he begins to experience his own feeling world. Thus, the baby's sense of self develops as he receives a mirrored response from his mother. Winnicott (1971) actually uses the term 'falling forever' to describe how it feels to lose experiences of holding and mirroring from the mother, and states that the baby will feel suddenly dropped.

This was evident in my work with three-year-old Jack, whom I hypothesized had absorbed sensations of the absence of holding from his birth mother prior to being removed from her care. On separation, he experienced further overwhelming feelings of abandonment, which he did not yet possess the mental resources to process and assimilate, but were evident in music therapy.

CASE VIGNETTE: **JACK, PART 1**

While choosing a beater/drumstick to play a drum, Jack rejected and dropped many beaters which he then refused to allow me to pick up. They remained lying on the floor, reminding me visually of the internal 'dropping' Jack had known. I interpreted his physical dropping as communicating his internal world expectation that he might be rejected and dropped by me. He was the one doing therefore doing the dropping first. Could he actually risk relationship with a music therapist? I avoided musically mirroring his loud crashing sounds because to do so might also have mirrored his felt sense of being dropped rather than holding it. Instead, I played gentle, soft, circling, repetitive chords.

Music therapy provided something very Winnicottian for Jack here, by opening up a less threatening space for relational play, while providing holding and mirroring for what emerged. Stern's (1998) concept of 'attunement' has similarities with Winnicott's (1971) 'mirroring', but can be seen as extending the idea. Attunement describes the processes by which 'a mother tracks, then reflects back to her infant, her sense of having shared in her infant's feeling state' (Wright 2009, p.22). It is essentially non-verbal and spontaneous, and relatively outside the mother's awareness, differing subtly from mirroring as it is more continuous and communicative. Stern proposes that the mother does not simply 'copy' or mirror, but rather captures, transposes and gives back a felt sense to the baby of being met and understood, which is perhaps similar to Bion's concept of containment.

CASE VIGNETTE: **JACK, PART 2**

For an entire session, Jack delighted in throwing any and every instrument available. He engaged in a repeated process of finding an instrument, picking it up, looking at it briefly, considering its musical usage, then throwing it to the floor. He never played a note of music. The experience of watching and listening was overwhelming, as Jack communicated over and over how dropped he had felt. I listened in a deeply embodied way, bearing witness to his experience.

Jack's nameless feelings of being dropped and falling forever had not been contained, held, mirrored or attuned to in his early life, and were now acted out in destruction in the room, which additionally served to cut him off from being able to really play in a musical relationship. Stern (2004) describes the embodied relational matrix in which humans remain embedded, and Jack could not escape his embodied memories, and required them to be met. Although unable to play himself, Jack could know himself in my music (which became a background resonant response) as contained, mirrored and attuned to.

Winnicott's (1960) concept of holding and Bion's (1963) concept of containing are among the most well-known and important contributions to psychoanalytic thought by these analysts. I have described how I have come to understand and use them in music therapy within adoption. I believe these concepts have value to music therapists in forming a theoretical base for adoption work because the music played in the therapeutic relationship with adoptees is similar to the musical non-verbal interactions of early life, providing an audible shape to emotional experience which can reveal unconscious trauma and internalized patterns of relating. Bion's containing offers an explanation for how the processing of early encounters in the lived emotional experience of clients might be one function of the music therapist. Winnicott's holding is more of an ontological concept that is primarily concerned with being and its relationship to time. Holding can happen within the medium of music, which of course has a temporal existence.

Winnicott's concept of 'going on being' additionally helps explain the language of movements that give form and allow for the sharing of vitality effects in musical relationships. In music therapy within adoption, these concepts combined enable an understanding of the nature of adoptees' pre-linguistic emotional experience and expression. Then, by accessing the adoptees' unconscious internal worlds, enduring impacts might be modified through new experiences of musical attunement. As relational patterns emerge gradually and tentatively, adoptees can be enabled to experiment playfully with different ways of relating. This can facilitate reparation of familial relationships which have been negatively impacted by attachment styles (Gravestock 2018), and adoptees and adopters alike might be supported in their struggle and sense-making about themselves and their familial relationships.

Suggested additional reading on attachment theory

Beebe, B. and Lachmann, F.M. (2013) *The Origins of Attachment: Infant Research and Adult Treatment*. New York, NY: Routledge.

Bowlby, J. (1969) *Attachment and Loss: Volume 1: Attachment*. London: Pimlico.

Fear, R.M. (2017) *Attachment Theory: Working Towards Learned Security*. London: Karnac.

Holmes, P. and Farnfield, S. (2014) *The Routledge Handbook of Attachment: Theory*. New York, NY: Routledge.

Owen, I.R. (2017) *On Attachment: The View from Developmental Psychology*. London: Karnac.

Chapter 4

Accessing Music Therapy

THE ADOPTION SUPPORT FUND

The Adoption Support Fund – accessing music therapy since 2015

Prior to the government establishing the Adoption Support Fund in May 2015, access to any sort of therapeutic support for adopted children and their families was varied across England, Scotland and Wales, and dependent entirely on local authority funding and availability. There was considerable inequity nationally, and little formulation regarding what might or should be available for families seeking therapeutic support. In 2015, the Adoption Support Fund (ASF) was created to enable equitable therapeutic funding for adoptive families. This chapter describes the frameworks that exist now for accessing music therapy (a recognized provision) via the ASF and how music therapy can be sought and obtained.

The ASF is an independent fund that was set up by the government in response to an identified need arising from the lived experience of families. Adoptive parent groups had pressed government because of the needs they had in placement which were being variously met. Adoption groups reported lived experience of inequitable access to therapy, citing some areas where local authorities did not have any access to funding for therapy that was specific to adoption, and others where there were only resources to provide very limited periods of therapy (often just six weeks). The ASF model was therefore based on an existing statutory framework for the assessment of adoption support, which had itself been previously experienced as woefully inadequate by many families in their feedback to adoption support services. The new ASF model endeavoured to address such inadequacies.

All local authorities and regional adoption agencies in the UK are now (since 2015) registered to apply to the ASF for help with therapy costs. The fund is available for any adopted children from the point at which they are placed with their adoptive families, up to the age of 21 (or even 25 if they possess an education, health and care plan). There is no funding available for children to access therapy prior to placement, so no real possibility to use the ASF for preparatory work, even with a placement that is anticipated to be difficult for identified reasons. In such cases, the local authority may be given extra resources to support the proposed placements of children deemed 'hard to place'. These may be children who are identified as demonstrating particular behavioural difficulties, or children who have disabilities, or children who are seeking placement as sibling groups. However, there are issues for music therapists considering working with children who have not yet had their permanent placement confirmed and ratified legally. A much hoped-for placement may not come into being, and children can be left trying to manage feelings about why that placement did not materialize. There is no funding source available in these situations, and children remain in foster or other placements possibly without their therapist being able to stay alongside them and support them to manage what has happened. This is another reason why permanency should precede therapy, or we risk giving children repeated experiences of abandonment.

When the ASF first came into being, families could apply for access to seemingly unlimited funds. It was evident that the government had not appreciated how many families would want and need to access the fund, and this itself was evidence of the large number of families who were struggling to manage the difficulties of adoption. Clearly, in the outworking of placements made then, 'love' was proving to be not enough (Chapter 1). A cap was put on funding due to the immense demand on resources. During 2018, this was set at a maximum of £2500 per child *per year* available for specialist assessments, and a further £5000 for therapy (and these amounts remain the agreed amounts until the end of financial year 2020 to 2021; the government have committed some funding for the 2021–22 financial year in advance of their spending review, because they recognize that absence of certainty regarding continuing funding is a major concern for families). As the budget is calculated yearly, it is possible for music therapists who are working with a child and family to put forward a case to the local authority and the ASF that work should continue beyond one year, and if necessary they should be able to access additional years of funding. When the need is argued for on the grounds of a child's therapeutic need, therapists do not report experiences of being denied continuing funds. The ASF recognizes in practice that for many families, long-term work will be required. This is why it is imperative that music therapists working within adoption are fully appraised of the nature of working with attachment and trauma and are able to argue coherently the reasons why families should be able to access long-term work. It is also incumbent on us not to engage in short-term work where we feel that to do so could be to the child's detriment. It can be worse for a child to have short-term interventions that mean a music therapist quickly enters and leaves their life, thus replicating their early experiences of abandonment. In the case of some children with complex needs, I have been enabled to provide very long-term therapy (over a number of years). Most cases have received work of a year's duration as a recommended minimum, some have received three years, and a few have entered their fourth year and beyond.

The local authority (LA) or regional adoption agency (RAA, usually an organization such as Coram, Barnardo's, Adoption UK, or Families First) that places a child with a family is responsible for assessing that same family's support needs for a total of three years after the adoption order is made. After three years, the responsibility then lies with the LA or RAA where the family now lives, if the child was placed in a different area from where they were living, or if the adoptive family have moved. For example, in my own area of practice (which in the Midlands has access to multiple county boundaries), a family may adopt with Leicestershire LA and be funded for therapy via the adoption support team in Leicester, but then move to Derbyshire five years after placement and then access funding for therapy via Derbyshire LA. Or, a family may adopt in a London LA and move to Leicester a year after the adoption order, and still be funded by the London LA until they are three years on from the adoption. A family may adopt through an RAA such as Coram but then receive additional therapeutic support via the LA area in which they live within three years of the adoption order. The ASF will fund therapeutic support for families who have chosen to adopt independently from abroad, or in other more unusual circumstances, but a fuller LA assessment of need may be required. There are currently various ways to adopt a child in the UK, and each specific family should be treated according to their presenting needs at whatever stage they are at post-adoption order and post-placement. Music therapists need to be clear about how the funding will be provided as the LA and ASF work together, but in day-to-day practice it is the LA who will be in direct contact with the music therapist.

CASE VIGNETTE: **RACHEL** AND **PETER**

Rachel and Peter had liaised to adopt their three children with Leicestershire LA. The children were placed, and the new family accessed the ASF through Leicestershire post-adoption services. They moved to a new home for their children to attend secondary school just three miles away, but in the catchment area of Derbyshire LA. A new application to the ASF through Derbyshire post-adoption services was made, and a smooth transition was managed by their therapist who was able to work across the county boundary.

When music therapists work with the ASF they need to establish good relationships with LA post-adoption support teams. It will be the post-adoption support service manager who will be available to the family and who will require the music therapist's assessment, interim reports and final evaluation of any work provided.

CASE VIGNETTE: **EMMA**

Emma lived in Camden when she adopted her seven-year-old son, but moved to Leicestershire to be near her family to help her with care during school holidays while she worked. As she was only a year post order and placement, her funding with the ASF was provided via Camden LA. Her music therapist in London was able to liaise in advance with a music therapist in Leicestershire and a handover period was agreed so that Emma's son did not experience the sudden loss of his first therapist. The second therapist had to establish a new working relationship with Camden post-adoption services to provide information on how music therapy was progressing.

Providing support to some adoptions can mean a music therapist having to travel to liaise with post-adoption services.

CASE VIGNETTE: **MIKE** AND **PHILLIPE**

Mike and Phillipe had adopted their sons in France some years previously, through a French adoption charity. They moved to England and were experiencing extreme difficulties with their eldest son who was excluded from school. They approached Leicestershire LA for support and an application was made through the ASF, and therapy was funded.

CASE VIGNETTE: **TIM** AND **MEI-LING**

Tim and Mei-Ling had chosen to adopt their daughter Changchang directly from China. They were living in the UK themselves, but Mei-Ling had Chinese heritage and wanted to adopt a baby girl from China. They had not been involved with any LA adoption service. When they began to experience some difficulties in placement, they approached their LA who were able to access funding through the ASF.

Some children may have specific cultural needs arising from their pre-adoption narrative, and again it is important to explore the processes that led to an adoption which may be impacting on the placement. In the case example above, Mei-Ling was able to give her daughter access to the British Chinese community, but also the family worked hard to fund return visits to China where Changchang could feel a connection with her place of birth.

In the past, a family would apply for therapeutic support directly with the LA and be assessed in terms of perceived need and then receive whatever funding was available. Now, however, families may themselves approach the ASF directly, and as their first point of contact. They do not have to go via a social worker to initially contact the ASF, but will see on accessing the website that they are directed to contact their local relevant LA or RAA who will support them and organize a formal request to the ASF once their needs have been assessed. (The ASF has contacted all LAs and RAAs and registered them for the ASF application portal.) The LA/RAA must then assess a family's support needs and apply to the ASF for suitable therapeutic support for that family within three months of the assessment. The family and LA/RAA will then search for a therapist who can work with the needs defined (often choosing to purchase support from their own list of approved suppliers) and obtain a quote for the work from an identified therapist. Some LAs request that families have three separate quotes, but this is not always the case. The element of competition for cheaper quotes is not experienced as helpful when we are advocating for the best care for families. The LA, in the guise of the post-adoption support team, will then formally apply to the ASF and, once funding is agreed, therapy will commence.

Music therapy (along with other creative therapies) is listed as an approved creative therapy for ASF funding. Some LAs keep a list of approved music therapists they can draw on, and certainly the LAs I predominantly work with are now building up their experience of which therapists are best placed to deal with which families. Part of the extended role of music therapists developing an adoption practice often needs to be to directly contact managers of local post-adoption services and inform them of their presence in the area as a music therapist specialized in adoption work. The ASF's own literature does advise that all self-employed/freelance therapists do this, as obviously not all LAs will be aware of local music therapists, and many may not have teams that are aware of music therapy or its relevance to adoption.

In order to provide an adoption music therapy service for the ASF, it is usually required that the therapist is registered with Ofsted, or alternatively a therapist can be employed to provide adoption support services under the Ofsted registration of the LA that is applying for funding. There are differences between LAs, but these tend to be slight. In my own practice, I am a registered and identified specialist therapist for one LA, and a consultant and specialist for two other LAs. The process of becoming a registered therapist who may be used by the ASF consists of the usual checks that any therapist would expect from an employer (such as the Disclosure and Barring Service check, evidence of qualifications, evidence of UK work status). In addition, most LAs will want to know the therapist's experience to date (usually provided in a CV) and may request an interview with the therapist, especially to assess their level of experience/further training in working with adoption, attachment and trauma. Once a therapist is registered on an LA list, they do not become an employee. The ASF is the direct funder of work via the LA, and work usually continues without any additional requirement to report to the LA. LAs also vary in their requirements for what they expect of music therapists during the work (for example, one LA I work with requests a brief written assessment of the family's need and what work is planned to happen at the outset of therapy, a further halfway report to evaluate how the work is going, and an end report when the agreed number of sessions is reached). Report writing can be a helpful way to provide a rationale and justification for the continuation of music therapy. An 'ending' report at the agreed limit of a series of sessions may actually recommend that therapy should continue long term, and if so there is no requirement for an identified piece of work to end and re-start. All adoption professionals working in the broader team supporting music therapy are well aware of the difficulty a lack of continuity can present for families already struggling with attachment and trauma-related issues.

In my own practice, I often find my initial contact comes direct from a family. They may have read about the ASF or been otherwise informed about it via friends who have used it, or from adoption support groups they attend. Families will be told of the existence of the ASF while going through the adoption process and are reminded of it later when first beginning to present their struggles. A parent may well decide they would like to access music therapy because they are aware of it, or because someone they know has had a positive experience of it, or they personally feel it might benefit a child who 'likes music'. As stated earlier, however, they may have little knowledge about why it might help, and what 'good' or appropriate music therapy might look like. Parents can obtain music therapists' contact details either directly from the British Association for Music Therapy (BAMT) or via their LA's own list of approved adoption therapists.

At this point of first contact (usually a telephone call or email from a parent), there will need to be some discussion with the parent/s about what music therapy is, and how it may help adopted children and their families. If the parent then wishes to go ahead to apply for funding and request work with a music therapist, they should be advised to contact their LA adoption support team in order to have the necessary initial 'assessment of need'. Experience in practice is that this usually happens quickly, and therapists will then be contacted by their local post-adoption support team to inform them that their LA is assessing a family who have requested music therapy with them. Once this assessment is complete (again, usually within just a few weeks), and the LA and parents agree that music therapy via adoption support is needed, the LA can apply directly to the ASF for funding. Again, LAs may differ in how they involve a chosen therapist. However, therapists are usually involved from this point on, and will be asked to contribute a funding estimate for the post-adoption team worker who compiles the request to the ASF. This estimate will detail the duration of session time, and how many proposed sessions might be required, as well as any room hire fee and travel costings. Some LAs insist that a brief description of any aims of the therapy is completed from the outset, and this will be done in conjunction with parents.

CASE VIGNETTE: **CATRINA**

One August, a music therapist received a telephone call from Catrina. Catrina had adopted Herbie who had mild cerebral palsy, and who she admitted she was finding it hard to attach to. She had approached a social worker who had suggested she had 'personal issues' which stopped her from attaching. She didn't feel that individual therapy for herself would help her understand her relationship difficulties with him, and via a friend at a disability play group she had heard about music therapy. Herbie liked playing instruments at nursery and Catrina felt happier engaging with him when playing music. She had found the music therapist's details on the BAMT website. The music therapist spoke for a while with Catrina about her initial decision to adopt a child with disability, and the difficulties she had experienced to date. The music therapist went on to explain how music, drawing on elements known as 'communicative musicality', might help improve her own relating with her son. Catrina was enthusiastic to engage in some work that didn't view her as being the problem because she couldn't attach and that sought to recognize and explore the complexities of relating within adoption. Catrina contacted the local adoption support team, with the music therapist as her chosen therapist. The LA contacted the music therapist, and together they applied for some sessions of joint child and parent music therapy. The ASF agreed to 20 weeks of work initially.

It is apparent from the above vignette that Catrina had lived experiences of negativity, blame and judgement when trying to seek help for the adoptive placement of Herbie. In contrast, even in the initial interactions with a music therapist that were about signposting her to obtaining ASF funding, the ground was being laid for attachment-informed music therapy that would hold her lived experience also.

CASE VIGNETTE: **KAREN** AND **TOM**

Karen and Tom had adopted sisters Maria and Phoebe who seemed to have few difficulties until they reached school age. Both children then seemed to have learning issues, though there was no apparent history of learning disability within their birth family. Contact with their adoption placement social worker led to them learning that the girls might well be presenting with features of foetal alcohol syndrome (which was not known about as a possible risk at the time of placement as their birth mother had refused to co-operate with any adoption assessment and was contesting their removal). Karen and Tom were angry that they didn't know about this prior to adopting and felt 'cheated' by the placing social worker. They felt new knowledge of the girls' more profound anticipated difficulties was causing them to reject their children. They contacted a music therapist, as a friend in their post-adoption social group had previously received music therapy and told them about it, so they looked up music therapists on the LA list of therapists. Their LA agreed to request funding from the ASF and they were granted 29 weeks of family work.

Sometimes, as in the case of Karen and Tom, families have developed difficult relations with support services such as their social worker. Such difficulties may also speak about the life trajectory of adopted children (in this case, the painful narrative of these sisters being likely affected by maternal alcohol use and other negative lived experience in their birth family, as well as the story of a non-relinquishing birth mother). These lived experiences, known later in placement, can come as a shock and new aspects of children's histories can be difficult to make sense of. The social worker had not deliberately withheld information, but it had not been accessible at the time of placement. Tom was very troubled by what he understood about foetal alcohol syndrome, and Karen was anxious that the girls may seek out their birth mother and learn that she did not want to give them up, and express a desire to return to her. Their worst fantasies were being expressed and impacting on relationships.

CASE VIGNETTE: **PAUL**

Paul had a 17-year-old adopted son, Alex, who was keen to trace his birth family when he became 18. Paul's adoption of Alex was described as 'plain sailing' and he hoped music therapy might help his son manage any contact with his birth family, which Paul knew would likely re-evoke trauma. Paul was aware of music therapy as he taught art at a university and an art therapist colleague suggested that creative arts therapies might help Alex. Previously, Alex refused to go to verbal counselling or psychotherapy because he stated he had no memories of living with his birth family and didn't know what he was supposed to talk about. In an initial telephone conversation, a music therapist explained to Paul how music can help access unconscious lived experience. The music therapist suggested that starting work at this point and building a safe confidential relationship with Alex might help in the coming months, when Alex might feel less able to talk with Paul. Paul agreed and said that Alex had said he might cause upset by tracing his birth family. Paul contacted his LA and an application was made to the ASF, which especially recognized this critical transitional time for adoption, and therefore agreed funding beyond the age of 18.

The music therapist in this case was able to identify some of the material underlying Paul's request on behalf of Alex, and was aware of the likely issues for an adoptee who is thinking of tracing a birth family, and how these may play out in lived experience.

The organization Adoption UK states that 16 per cent of applications to the ASF to date have been for music therapy. This is a smaller percentage than for other creative arts therapies but music therapy is nonetheless maintaining a steady presence. One of the regional adoption agencies, First4Adoption, which accesses music therapy on behalf of children it places, has the following statement on its website for those who might require information on why music therapy can be helpful:

> Music therapy can help children from complex and traumatic backgrounds in a range of ways. It can help to increase concentration and attention skills, improve family and social relationships, and

increase a child's confidence. For many children, it is the first step towards finding ways of dealing with their feelings of loss, frustration and emotional trauma so that they can start to learn to trust, love and lead happier lives.[1]

This simple yet informative statement is useful for families at the outset of their journey of seeking therapeutic resources to help them both manage and think about the difficulties their adopted children are experiencing. The statement first defines the sorts of problems a parent may present their child with, such as attention, social skills, and so on. It then touches on the feelings that will underlie behaviour, and pre-adoption experiences such as trauma and loss which, although perhaps not conscious to an adopted child or known to a parent, are still exerting an effect. Often families need helping gradually towards an understanding of the enduring impact of early life experience, which can be hard to grasp, especially if an adoptee was placed at a very young age.

In 2015, I was asked to write the literature on adoption for the British Association for Music Therapy. Adoptive families can access this leaflet for advice about music therapy for adoption difficulties, and the information can also be found in Appendix 2 of this book. The leaflet aims to deepen understanding of what music therapy is, but also to provide more complex descriptions of the ways in which early trauma might manifest, and how research has helped in understanding this.

It is often difficult for families to believe something about their child that they cannot see, and it can be useful to draw on the growing body of evidence from neuroscience to help families into understandings. Evidence from fMRI scans can help parents develop their understanding of the impact on the developing brain and the mind-body of all kinds of trauma. This information can then help them to develop increased empathy for their child, who they may have previously seen as being deliberately 'naughty' and not related this behaviour in any way to their being adopted. Parents may struggle when they feel they have given their child 'everything' and yet still their child wants to seek out a birth family or is

---

1   www.first4adoption.org.uk

acting in ways that the adoptive family finds difficult and beyond familial experience.

'Journey' is a word perhaps overused in therapy worlds, and yet one which is extremely applicable to adoption. The adoption community refers to the lifelong journey of adoption because it seems to best describe the process that children and families experience from the point of placement, for the rest of their lives. Children who have been removed, often at a very young age, have no knowledge of how their life began nor the decisions that were made which turned their life around and set it on a new path. Adopters come often to adopt on the back of their experiences of infertility and so on that have meant they could not come to parent in any other way than adoption. A new family is put together hopefully, and it is often only gradually over time that difficulties emerge. Then the enduring effects of pre-adoption trauma are witnessed, or parents are reminded of their own pain and loss. As children grow and develop, things may go very well for a long time, and difficulties might only arise at particular transitions such as adolescence. Or problems may exist from day one. Either way, both children and families will find themselves in positions and situations that they could not have anticipated. It can be an enormously humiliating task for parents to seek help, to admit to perceived 'failings', and to access therapy. Families continue a journey of learning more about themselves and their experiences and about the lifelong effects of early life experience, especially trauma. A music therapist's journey with a family begins at the point of first contact, which could well be an ostensibly simple discussion about accessing the ASF. It is imperative, then, that as music therapists we remain aware of and open to the struggles that arise in adoptive placements, and can support families to access the help they will need if an adoption is to endure and relationships are to improve. This necessitates an openness to the lived experience of each family member, and a sensitive holding of varying lived experiences as they unfold and are made evident in the work.

All content pertaining to the ASF is available under the Open Government Licence v3. The website for the ASF is reached via www.gov.uk, under 'Adoption Support Fund' which comes under the

Department for Education. The ASF can also be contacted on 01223 463517 and at as@mottmac.com.

Adoption support can be accessed from local authority social services under the children's social care and supporting families teams in county councils.

Chapter 5

Referral Presentations

A NEEDS-LED APPROACH FOR DIVERSE ISSUES

As the previous chapters have illustrated, adoption is a lifelong aspect of identity. Working with adoptees and their families is complex and rich because the multiple narratives that lead to placement involve multiple losses interacting in all manner of ways during the outworking of family life over many years. We have seen that an *adoption panel* places children, but rarely sees the longer-term consequences of the decisions that are made. As *music therapists*, we hear these ongoing stories and learn how, if adoptive families are not supported with services shaped by an understanding of trauma and attachment, early life experiences are re-enacted, at worst resulting in family crisis/adoption breakdown. We will now join families at a point of stress and difficulty, known as 'a referral'. This deceptively simple descriptor is in fact a nodal point of the overall experience of the adoption through time, and all that has accumulated and is now being expressed.

The lifelong nature of adoption means that uncomfortable and unresolved feelings can be stirred up for any member of an adoptive family at any point in their journey. There is no point at which it can be stated it is more or less likely for placement difficulties to arise, but any transition (such as a child starting school, or changing school, or moving to a new house, or experiencing the death of a grandparent) can evoke feelings of loss and resonate with earlier attachment material. Implicit emotional and somatic memories evoked by association to past events are not always recognizable as memories as such. Rather, adoptees re-experience the feeling of being traumatized without knowing what unconscious memory their feelings are linked to. Bodies and emotions remember events for which there are no words to describe or visual images to recall. Some families report that their family life had been content for many years, until perhaps some transitional juncture resonated with earlier lived experience (in children or parents). This will have resulted either in troubling 'acting out' in an adopted child, which led the family to seek out professional help, or presentations in the parents such as depression, which was linked (obviously or more obliquely) to the adoption history.

CASE VIGNETTE: **MARNIE**

Marnie came to music therapy aged 18. She described a positive experience of having been adopted, and good relationships with her adoptive family. She experienced no difficulties throughout childhood, but in recent months had begun having episodes she called 'the jumps'. These began when she was travelling on a bus and hadn't seen someone sit down behind her, and when they made a sound she was startled and jumped, but excessively. Further episodes occurred and she had become concerned she was 'going crazy'. Her parents thought she may be developing an anxiety disorder. Marnie had begun to trace her birth family, and in the process of learning about them she discovered that both parents had been severely misusing drugs prior to her being removed aged six weeks. With her music therapist, Marnie was able to explore thinking about the baby's startle response, and recognized that when she was a baby there would have been little that mediated between her and the world. She was able to recognize that her 'jumps' now mimicked the early startle response, and that her body remembered her early life. Giving this new meaning to the behaviour helped Marnie and her adopters deal kindly with it and it stopped manifesting shortly after.

There are obvious transitional moments in a child's life where such resonances might be predicted and planned for. Supportive interventions can be put in place in advance around these times. Some transitions are obvious to spot in terms of the associations they might carry, but others less so. For many families, their child starting school was a potent reminder to that child of abandonment, and resulted in separation anxiety that led to referral. Other major transitions such as a house move, or a bereavement, can stir up feelings pertaining to adoption, even if the connection may not be instantly recognizable. Holidays that have resonances of family times, such as Christmas and Easter (for example), can be very painful for children who may fantasize about their birth family and have notions of idealized families aroused because Christmas especially is a time when the emphasis is on family life and emotional expectations are high. It can be a challenge on a yearly basis, or perhaps it is only in one particular year when difficulties come to the fore.

Regularly adoptive families report that birthdays are incredibly difficult, when children are reminded that they have a birth family somewhere, and when they may ask again why they had to be adopted. Also, adoptive parents may find that their child's birthday is a reminder to them that they are not their child's flesh and blood parent. Their child was born, yet they were not present. A birthday may bring back reminders of an adoptive parent's own inability to become pregnant, which can often go unrecognized (as there is no social grieving process for such circumstances) and which may be acted out in other ways. Birthdays can also evoke memories of any birth children a family had who have died, and adopted children can tune into the emotions around such circumstances very easily, even if these are not articulated. Renewed awareness of the reality of a birth family somewhere 'out there' at birthday times might activate fears of the adopted child tracing their birth family at the age of 18. Some adoptive parents believe their children will end contact with their adoptive family once they are 'reunited' with their birth family, especially if their child has regularly told them this is a plan they have, as some children do. Birthdays then, constructed as happy celebratory times, can be anything but for adoptees and their families.

Other circumstances become very different routes to seeking referral for music therapy. Younger children quite early on in a placement may be presented as lacking a meaningful engagement/

attachment with their adoptive parents. Parents may desperately need some feedback emotionally from their child and when the child is unable to respond, then they may be described as 'unable to attach'. Other children may be presented early in the life of their adoption placement when the placement is not yet felt to be in difficulty, but where there are psychological issues that a family need more support with. Children who are known to have experienced abuse and additional trauma may be referred in anticipation of difficulties. Adopters who have taken children who are born disabled and subsequently rejected by their birth family because of disability may request help in relation to specific disability issues. The child's disability is forever conflated with adoption and identity issues, and although the presenting referral may have a disability focus, adoption needs to be thought about too. Combining abuse and disability, adopters may have a child who is disabled/brain injured not from birth but as a result of having been physically abused in their birth family. They may present also with disability issues, but these will be conflated in a complex way with a trauma narrative which resulted in the child's removal.

Some adoptees are babies who were born as the result of rape, and families may present wanting to know how to support their child in age-appropriate ways as they become curious about their early beginnings. Young children, lacking words for their experiences, act them out behaviourally in a range of ways such as aggression (to parents, siblings, or in school and other settings), stealing, lying, bedwetting, self-harm, eating distress and so on. Sexually abused children may have gone on to offend sexually themselves, bringing 'shame' into the family and/or involving the criminal justice system. Older children may be truanting, sleeping rough and becoming involved in risky behaviours (such as alcohol and drug misuse, illegal driving, dangerous sports). Children may have been involved with CAMHS and even experienced hospitalization (for example, with anorexia or self-harm) where an adoption context is not obvious but may underlie a manifest mental health problem. At the point of referral, the presenting issue is likely to be therefore behavioural and a re-enactment through whatever means of trauma. Circumstances may have become so extreme, and family life so difficult for all concerned, that parents may have lost empathy with their child, and even be unwilling to consider the significance of the child's adoption trauma and how this might be influencing current behaviour.

A more general precursor to seeking support will be high levels of emotional and behavioural disturbance reported in adopted children which may not actually be manifest at all in the home context, and could be school-based. Adopted children are at a high risk of exclusion, especially if the school has not had access to attachment training. Parents will frequently report their children's lack of progress in school and an inability for the children to achieve at the desired level for their chronological age. This may be accompanied by 'disruptive behaviours', with threats of exclusion from school, and I have even encountered situations where schools will only keep children on roll if the family are actively seeking therapy.

All possible transitions and circumstances above could be situations that engender referral. The presentations described are diverse, but in my own practice the consistent main driver to seeking external support has been some sort of crisis point, perhaps brought about by some of the events (among many others) described above. In the most severe circumstances, it may have been mooted that the only solution to the crisis would be for the adoptee to be returned to the care system. Because referrals do not have the same genesis, each referral must be treated individually. This is especially true when parents are seeking help for the 'problem' as the presenting lived experience and identify it as such. They may then not be interested in accessing adoption and trauma-informed services and may indeed see professionals as colluding with their child in their 'naughtiness' and giving the child excuses for their behaviour. This is why music therapists need to be needs-led and work with each referral as its presentation best requires. At all times, a needs-led approach should be alive to the varying lived experiences within the family, and how differing 'truths' of a situation might be held together.

CASE VIGNETTE: **KAY**

Kay was referred for 'extreme behaviour problems' at the age of 15, including an unplanned pregnancy resulting in termination. She had been seen by her own GP initially, who informed adoptive parents that her behaviour was 'no different from any teenager' and that the pregnancy bore no relation to her adoption history but was part of her general disruptiveness. Kay was initially uncertain about having a termination and had discussed keeping her baby with her adoptive mother who was unwilling to provide a home for them both. At the abortion clinic, she had angrily said to her mother that 'anything was better than making a baby get adopted by someone like you'. After the abortion, Kay's mum reported that Kay's life went 'back to normal' and she showed no 'remorse'. However, her behaviour at home deteriorated some months later, and both parents became extremely angry with her.

During assessment, they informed me that they were reluctant to give her 'the excuse' of being an adopted child as a 'way out' of being reprimanded. Kay had been adopted at six weeks old, and up until her teenage years had been very contented, and her parents could see no reason for her acting out. Both parents had been extremely compliant teenagers themselves and had not experienced sexual relating until they married. They then struggled to conceive a baby, and when they did eventually become pregnant, Kay's adoptive mother had five miscarriages. Kay said that her mum constantly told her she was 'different' from her adoptive parents, and in arguments had described her as 'like a changeling' and 'just like her birth mother'. (Kay's birth mother had become pregnant as a teenager and relinquished Kay, resulting in adoption.)

In music therapy, Kay wanted to sing ballad-style pop songs and asked if I could accompany her on the piano. As we sat together, Kay would mimic the facial and body gestures of female pop stars, but would suddenly stop. She could not tolerate words that she said were 'too romantic and soppy...cos they make me feel sick'. I began to wonder if some lyrics of certain songs held too much resonance for Kay. Frequently the lyrics were of jilted lovers longing to be taken back. Was Kay unable to voice her heart's cry to be taken back by her birth mum? Was she also longing for her adopted mum to love her as she was? Simultaneously, was she grieving for the baby she had aborted, and recognizing that she and the baby were similar in that they had both been relinquished, to different ends? The songs Kay chose were structured for the most part by repeating chord sequences, which felt very containing. In time, instead of using actual songs, I made up similar but improvised circling chord sequences on the piano. Kay was able gradually to improvise a melodic line which she hummed over the top of this, and eventually put lyrics to her melody. At the age of 16 she created lyrics called 'Two Years Away', and although ostensibly this was a song about meeting and marrying someone who would know, love and understand her entirely, I sensed that it was a metaphor which was predicting her eventual search at 18 for her birth mother. In a later improvisation titled 'Be My Only Baby' she sang about a desire to be the 'only one' to someone, and this carried resonances of her needing to be her birth mother's 'only baby'. She was fearful her birth mum may have gone on as an adult to have and keep other children. It also was perhaps at another level a song for her own 'only' aborted baby. Kay's experiences leading to her presentation and referral to music therapy were very much related to her being an adopted baby, and this seemed to literally play out in her music and singing.

It is not unusual for families to be unable to construe their child's acting-out behaviours as being rooted in the child's early life experience. Some families may not have been in touch with adoption services or any adoption support groups for many years. Life may have continued just as any other form of family life with little regard to the lifelong nature of adoption. Therapy is required, however, not because the child has an attachment disorder that resides inside them, like an organic illness, but rather because the problems that are arising for the child have their origins in their earliest relationships. Attachments are about relationships. An attachment cannot happen in a vacuum, so although a child may have an attachment style that results from their experience (and which may not be compatible with their adopter's attachment style), any attachment disorder can only exist as it is played out in a relationship. When the perceived 'damage' to a child was relational, it can be posited a therapy that is relational can help repair disrupted and de-regulated ways of managing the self. It can take considerable preparatory work with a family to enable them to embrace ideas of what any music therapy might actually be 'about', and to accede that difficult behaviours in the here and now are a means of communicating distress that is located in the past.

Some families may manage the whole trajectory of childhood, and only present for music therapy when adoptees become young adults. Young people might initiate the search for therapeutic support themselves around the time of their 18th birthday, when they might want to trace their birth family. Some young adults are supported by their adoptive family to do so, but others may have been unable to even voice the desire to trace because of fears of hurting their adoptive parents, so this desire has been expressed implicitly instead. I have also worked with young adults no longer living in their adoptive family home, and sometimes with no ongoing contact with their adopters, but who are desirous of contact, recognizing the complexities that may have led to a breakdown of relationship. In one instance of working with a very elderly client with dementia, aspects of his distress were located back in early life. His lived experience of being relinquished as a baby was evoked for him when he was once more vulnerable and physically needing care in a nursing home, and 'abandoned' by his wife who could not cope with his demented state. The adoption journey clearly is lifelong, because trauma has left its imprint. Clients may be presented by those who care for them at any point during the life span, or present directly themselves. This is why it is important for therapists working in all areas of music therapy across the life span to hold an awareness of early life material and attachment in mind. There is no adoption-specific provision for adult adoptees within social care. Adult adoptees who inevitably go on to re-present may do so in other services such as mental health services, which may or may not be trauma and attachment informed. Throughout our lives, we all constantly experience new relationships and new losses, and these will inevitably evoke our own attachment histories. This is why as music therapists we should advocate for lifelong access to therapeutic support for adoptive families, given evidence from lived experience in the adoption community that earliest beginnings matter and continue to exert their influence.

When adoptive parents bring their children to music therapy, they regularly describe a sense of failure and shame. Parents believe they have not 'managed' to be a good adopter, and that they have let their child down. Yet adopters are tasked with helping adopted children to achieve healthy relating, emotional regulation and reflexive function, which is an enormous challenge. When additionally an adopter has their own unresolved feelings pertaining to their own lived experience, they too will need particular support with managing and exploring their own shame, guilt and perceived failure. On occasions, it might be necessary to refer an adopter for their own individual therapy separately, even if they are working in a dyad in music therapy with their child. An adopted child's experience as it is brought to light in music therapy can put an adoptive parent painfully in touch with their own childhood, family and adult relationships. Parents may therefore need additional work to enable them to contain their own feelings when they are present in the child's therapy, so as not to project or over-identify with their children.

Only if a parent is able to be in contact with and simultaneously contain their own lived experience will they be able to become fully and authentically available to their child as a secure parental base. This is especially true for adopters who were themselves adopted. (In Chapter 8, an example is given of a way that a mother and son found to deal with both of their experiences of being adopted.) Since the impact of parental attachment styles is influential in the development of those of their adopted children, this is crucial. As previous chapters have mentioned, parents may carry enduring loss pertaining to their own infertility, which may be compounded by feelings of disappointment in their adopted children who may not measure up to their fantasies or expectations.

Parents who have been constantly and solely in receipt of their children's enacted pain are carrying a huge emotional burden. Adopters can self-blame for their children's difficulties which have persistently endured many years beyond initial placement, even in the face of their 100 per cent love and commitment. It is difficult for everyone to recognize and become fully aware of the depth of a child's struggles resulting from their earliest life experiences.

Many parents report how their own shame has been worsened when they have felt blamed or judged by workers, including therapists. At the outset of music therapy, it is imperative that we do not attribute blame to either child or parent, but find ways to talk about trauma causing difficulties in the relational 'spaces between' people. It can take some time therefore to engender a therapeutic alliance, and to reassure adopters that a music therapist is not engaged in order to form judgements about their parenting, but rather to explore with the family what impacts on parenting adopted children. Helping parents to perceive their requirement for external professional involvement as a positive move might be the beginning of opening up explorations of parent-child intersubjectivity and discussions about why relating becomes so painful and difficult. Additional support around the family can build up adoptive parents' knowledge of matters such as attachment, neurobiology, intersubjectivity and so on. This may be likened to our need simultaneously as music therapists to have adoption-specific training in addition to our music therapy qualifications, in order to engage in an informed manner in adoption work. I will suggest to parents that they are the 'experts', as they will have been living with the material their child presents for a long time, and that I am joining them on the process of sense-making in order to alleviate some of the difficulties. Taking this sensitive stance informed by an adoption-specific perspective can lead to empathic understanding developing more in ourselves as music therapists, as we recognize how much sustained commitment in the face of difficulty and social isolation the family may have already come through in their search for the right supports. In their social lives, adoptive parents may have friendships with non-adoptive parents who may not understand the needs of adopted children and find interaction with the family difficult, and even give up on friendship. Adopters who seek help are once again placing themselves at the mercy of professionals, and sometimes the same professionals who they had to approach to be given permission to adopt in the first place. Help-seeking therefore can create enormous vulnerability in adopters, some of whom might need considerable reassurance to engage.

In Chapter 2, Delaney's (1998) description of an adoption crisis was mentioned, showing how a pattern of inevitable cyclical negative relating between child and adopter occurs, based on clashing internal worlds. Delaney describes some professionals as 'unthinking' when they blame adopters for 'failing' their children. It is incumbent on us then, as music therapists seeking to work in needs-led ways with families, to understand and appreciate the complicated 'relational dance' Delaney describes. We also need to hold stories of anger against other professionals, knowing that not all services a family has encountered will be adoption informed. This is not necessarily a form of 'pitting' one professional against another, polarized as 'bad' and ourselves as 'good', but is a recognition that not all are adoption, attachment and trauma informed.

Chapter 2, as well as identifying parental needs at referral, also showed how it is adoptees who most often carry the blame for placement failings, and who thereby generate referral. We met Alice, who was monitoring not only her own behaviour, but that of her three brothers. Rather than 'bad behaviour' generating referral, Alice's behaviour was overly 'good', to the point that parents were concerned about her. Alice felt that she had been blamed for not managing her siblings, who had been 'naughty' and disrupted their first adoption. We now hear a bit more of her narrative at referral, and how this impacted the early stages of music therapy.

CASE VIGNETTE: **ALICE**

Alice's adopters said she would never show her upset or anger with anyone. She was described as having developed a permanent smile and her parents felt she tried in all ways possible to present herself in all contexts as endearing and loveable. She would control any behaviour her siblings exhibited that she thought might be disruptive. If they cried she would 'shush' them and tell them to stop. If they were cross she would attempt to make them laugh. The children's first adoptive placement failed after only two weeks. She and her brothers had been very sad when they had to leave the home of their previous adopter. She had cried, and one of her brothers had shouted at their new adopters for 'stealing' them from their previous placement. She thought the placement had ended because of her brothers' 'naughtiness'. Her compliance, which in the early days of her individual music therapy was manifest in her playing of beautiful yet tightly controlled music, was indicative of her extreme anxiety. She would sit, crosslegged on the floor, and wait for me to suggest playing. She would then ask me what I wanted to play, and if I was oblique in my response she would become even more anxious as choosing for herself might risk choosing something I did not want or like to play. Her only desire was to keep me happy. Once we began to play together, she could never risk defining a tempo, or creating her own melody. She could not play unless I started and then she would exactly mirror my rhythms. She knew I played a violin and asked to learn violin at her school.

Unfortunately, when playing with her violin at home she had managed to break off a bow hair (a totally harmless event). She had been terrified then of getting the violin out at home in case her parents saw she had 'broken' it and sent her away again. Instead, she asked her mum if she could bring the violin to her music therapy session. Reluctantly, in the music therapy room, she opened the case, which in her mind would mean revealing to me (her only hoped for ally, who might secretly be able to repair the instrument) the damage she had caused. When she did open it, her panic was evident. For some time, she could not accept my assurance that bow hairs often break, and it felt important to help her to know this to lessen her extremely hyperaroused state. However, this instant provided a wonderful metaphor of 'broken instruments' for us to work with, and conversations about how hard it is to play when we fear something is damaged. After this difficult session (wherein neither of us played a note) the quality of our relating changed. Alice would attend and ask which instrument might be 'safe to break' in the session, and we worked with a keyboard without it's sustain pedal, a set of xylophone keys laid on the floor (rather than on their base), a recorder without its bottom section and so on. Alice quickly discovered how instruments could still function when they had been 'damaged' (or, as I reframed it, 'altered') but that we might need to 'listen differently'. This was a metaphor I was able to take back to her adoptive parents, and indeed Alice joined me in explaining to them that she was scared of showing how broken she had felt. She needed to know they would care for her and listen to her as the altered 'instrument' she now was.

At the juncture of referral, when families may be overwhelmed, in total pain and presenting in crisis and distress, therapists may increasingly be aware of being pressed for 'results'. Social workers will be anxious that the adoption may break down (because when a breakdown occurs, a resulting investigation has to take place). Children have sometimes been described to me as becoming too 'difficult', 'controlling', and 'naughty', even by social workers who might have placed them and be aware of their histories. If 'improvement' (in terms of 'outcome measures' and 'evaluation') cannot be shown, and indeed shown *quickly*, there are threats to both music therapist and the family of the therapy being discontinued because it is not 'doing anything'. Such punitive structures arise when systems are not able to bear the reality of the pain that histories of loss carry with them, and that subsequently this work takes time. Adopted children may sometimes need to get much 'worse' (in terms of the way that they articulate their distress) before they get better and they need music therapists who can go into the darkness with them and really stay there with them for a long time. Traumatic early experiences create a persistent darkness that families end up residing in, and as music therapists we must stay and stay and stay in darkness with them. Such practice often feels odd in a world where we are pressed to show evidence of 'resolved attachments' within a six-week block. Knox (2011) writes about the necessity of staying in the sharing of traumatic experience to establish different relationship forms that only *over time* can move towards integration. A *space to think* and a *time to think in*, then, are the first ingredients for families to feel contained enough to work safely.

It is to be hoped that legislative changes ensure the full extent of children's difficulties over the life span is acknowledged at the point of making placements and that therapeutic support is made available. The cyclical dance of relational difficulties will likely emerge in new families at some point. The lived experience of families highlights their need and desire for lifelong access to specialist adoption resources, which are informed by attachment and trauma awareness. Because the adoption narrative is one that endures for a person's life, families articulate a need for an accessible, flexible, enduring system wherein appropriate therapeutic resources can be accessed. Families refer themselves to music therapy at points often of desperate need. At the point of placement at the adoption panel they are led to believe therapeutic support will be available and accessible as required but this has not always been the case. The ASF has certainly reduced competition for therapeutic support and its very existence acknowledges that many more families than anticipated are presenting requests for therapy. However, as the previous chapter showed, the demands on the ASF have been great, highlighting an enormity of need that was not envisaged. It is imperative that as music therapists we take this rare current opportunity (while accessing the ASF and shaping its outworking is still a relatively new process) to shape services that are appropriate for our clients' needs, and insist on specialist adoption music therapy provision that is fit for purpose. Otherwise, if we do not manage to engage families at their varying points of referral, and sustain them through difficult times, they are likely to re-present, and their children on becoming young adults in time risk entering other services which are not adoption-specific.

Chapter 6

A Needs-Led Music Therapy Approach

LISTENING TO LIVED EXPERIENCE

In this chapter, I describe how my own approach to working in a needs-led way within the adoption community, based on lived experience of both my clients and myself as music therapist within that community, has evolved. It is impossible for one chapter to completely define and describe all the ideas that have influenced my practice over the past decade. Inevitably, influences include my own psychoanalytic music therapy training, then additional training courses I have since attended (specific to music therapy, adoption, attachment and trauma). For over a decade, I have also been influenced by consistent supervision, with the same supervisor I've had since qualifying. Supervision with a music therapist allows me to focus on musical relating, while considering theoretical perspectives that may help to account for the material discussed. Later, further influences came from conversations with my PhD supervisory team, who opened my work up to include discourses in addition to music therapy or psychotherapy, helping me to engage further philosophically in my own sense-making process. My lived experience of personal psychotherapy with a Jungian analyst/art therapist directed me to contemporary writing on trauma and attachment and especially concepts of relational psychotherapy, impacted by neuroscience. The greatest influence, however, has been the work itself, wherein children and their families have caused me to think anew, to challenge orthodoxy and to find ways of working that are relevant to making sense of their lived experience within the adoption community.

I am not defining here a 'model' by any means, but rather introducing concepts that have been useful for music therapy's development within the adoption community that I work in. The concepts I employ may not be familiar to other music therapists wanting to embark on adoption work. (Some concepts that I find especially helpful and use consistently are discussed in more depth in Chapter 3.) When we immerse ourselves in the communities within which we work, and aim to learn from these communities what is most helpful for them, we soon realize that there is no 'one size fits all' model. In an earlier book (Gravestock 2019a) I discussed how this approach, rather than a formalized 'method', privileges client processes of being and becoming (Sills 2008) which occur in the presence of a therapist who listens for the implicit, while witnessing and holding difficulties and dilemmas. My practice remains an incomplete jigsaw puzzle of therapeutic thought, which nonetheless forms a loose frame for thinking about music therapy for adoptees with trauma histories, and which is evolving still from continued clinical experiences and ongoing research. You, as the reader, are invited to think with me about theoretical positions and concepts I have found useful, but to develop and adapt your own practice as relevant after engagement with these ideas (which might be described as a philosophical overview of what constitutes a practice of music therapy within the adoption community).

My own practice has developed first and foremost from experiences of musical relating with clients. As an established adoption practitioner, I am often asked what training I did to become competent within the area before starting, and what skills might someone need who wished to develop similar work. I cannot answer this simply or easily, nor suggest any 'techniques' that can be easily applied. This is because my practice and approach began simply with my belief that music therapy had something to offer in the field of adoption, and then continued to gradually develop into a practice that is felt by the community as being most helpful to them. As I am a member of that community, it has inevitably meant ongoing development of myself. For anyone wishing to set up work of this nature, I recommend also considering personal therapy that can enable you to work with clients who will draw on all of your own attachment experiences.

As I discussed to some extent in the Preface, when I embarked on my first (tentative and definitely faltering) clinical work as a music therapist in adoption, I drew on:

- my own training in psychoanalytic music therapy
- my previous experience as a CAMHS adoption clinician
- my previous family therapy training
- core principles of attachment theory
- increasing knowledge of contemporary theories of attachment
- other associated training/courses
- wide reading around the area
- engagement with the adoption community as an adoption panel member.

This is a music therapist's lived experience and incorporates my own trajectory of learning and practising. It has all impacted on me at a cognitive level, and yet thinking about our work is only one aspect of being a music therapist. Supervision highlighted other aspects, as did personal therapy. Experiencing therapy for myself that drew on contemporary awareness of a psychoanalytic, relational, trauma-informed approach offered perhaps the greatest learning for me and provided a framework for what I might offer in my own work. Becoming a so-called specialist has been far less about developing a 'theoretical model' and much more about developing myself as a musical, embodied, thinking primary 'tool' to do the work. Descriptions in this chapter of elements I have encountered on the way might act as a guide to those who want to develop similar practice.

Developing any musical relationship involves both listening to and playing with our clients. It sounds so simple and obvious, and yet as I learned about embodied therapy (Rothschild 2000; Van der Kolk 2014; Totton 2015), I realized that we cannot play music other than with our bodies. Music is not a tangible, visible object but is experienced as a temporal, acoustic form that is played with, heard by, and felt within the body. The philosopher Maurice Merleau-Ponty (1945/1965) describes how we can only ever perceive and know the world subjectively through the body, and, even more strikingly, Heidegger (Heidegger *et al.* 1927/1962) states '*We* hear, not the ear'. More deeply, in fact, than even physical bodies or ears hearing, entire *beings* hear. When we engage in listening to a client within a music therapy session, listening is not just a prelude to our 'therapeutic response', nor is it a 'technique' among 'techniques', but rather listening – truly, deeply, embodied listening – is 'our most primordial way of being with and bearing with another human being in pregnant silence' (Wilburg 2013, p.8). As music therapists, if we are endeavouring to offer needs-led practice, we ourselves need to become comfortable with listening to our clients, without playing ourselves, and also to listening to silences. There should not be a need to fill every space in the session with music. Wilburg (ibid.) continues, 'we cannot really be with others in silence unless we can bear ourselves in this silence…to be and embody our being' (p.53). This is why it is imperative that we consider how we are able to 'bear' ourselves first and foremost, before we are able to 'bear' our client as well, becoming present and listening to all they bring.

It is this 'deep listening' that has felt essential for adoptees to experience, as an initial way of having their 'being' recognized. I will devote a considerable amount of this chapter to exploring Wilburg's concepts because his attention to listening (a core aspect of what music therapists do) has significance for adoption. Wilburg advocates a therapeutic approach known as 'philosophical counselling', which he describes as 'an embodied philosophical psychology of listening' (2013, p.10). I borrow from this approach to form my own definition of how I listen to adoptees and have since described as 'an embodied musical attachment informed listening'.

Wilburg unites Heidegger's (Heidegger *et al.* 1927/1962, see Chapter 7) philosophical understanding of listening with the psychological understanding of thinking developed by the

Independent (or Middle) Group of psychoanalysts in Britain (a group of which Winnicott eventually became a member). Wilburg's work therefore chimes with mine as I attempt to unite aspects of classical psychoanalytic theory with aspects of attachment theory, and new thinking in relational analysis. He describes how a deeper way of listening to self and others might be developed, which I liken to a musician's continued sense of their own embodied playing, and the way this is used in listening relationships within music therapy. Wilburg suggests that 'the more people write about what Heidegger said…the less they attempt to embody what he did…in particular his way of listening' (p.11). Similarly, this book's description of what I have developed is only useful if other music therapists immerse themselves in their own clinical experiences and make sense of what emerges in conjunction with their own clients in embodied relating. Wilburg says that his model attempts to 'conserve a way of thinking and listening that can be experienced, explored, and embodied *but never institutionalized*' (p.11). As such, his approach fits with my own descriptor of music therapy practice which instead of providing a set of frameworks, skills, methods and techniques, opens out a space to encourage others to engage in sense-making of their own work. This is not easy to summarize as a model or set of techniques and as such cannot be 'institutionalized'.

Wilburg's approach, then, focuses on the 'inner bearing of both counsellor and client' (p.16), which is what my own approach encourages. What does this mean for a music therapist? In intersubjective relating there are two people, and often only the client is written about, yet the music therapist's 'inner bearing' is of equal importance, especially when we are engaging with material around attachment and loss. (Chapter 9 of this book is devoted to the role of the therapist within intersubjectivity.) When working as music therapists, it is impossible for us to separate listening from our being because when we listen our whole being is involved, and this whole being is also communicated back to our client. This is unavoidable *whether we recognize and pay attention to it or not*. If we hope to attune to another individual via listening we cannot hide ourselves away because our body will convey the essential tone of our own being. This becomes (in Wilburg's language) a 'carrier wave on which messages are not only received but also transmitted wordlessly by the listener' (p.16). Listening (a basic core element of our practice) is never neutral.

Interestingly, Wilburg uses a musical analogy to make his point:

> In music, a single note or chord might tremble with a certain incompleteness and in this sense quest a response from an answering chord or note. There are no verbal questions and answers in a piece of music, and yet we hear in its tones a constant questing and response. The same is true of the music of feeling. *It is through tones of feeling that we quest an answering response, not in words but from answering tones that communicate*...not *in* but *through*. (p.26; emphasis added)

Some of the neuroscience of music and its effects on the brain go some way to explaining how these 'tones of feeling' happen, but such description can only ever be partial. Science provides hard evidence, yet lacks explanation for the soul of both music itself and musical 'tones of feeling' occurring in music therapy.

Music can be described technically in detailed terms of its elements, and the physics of such elements. Similarly, emotions can be technically and scientifically shown to alter when an fMRI scan is taken of the brain. But although both these processes offer a description of *what* happens, they cannot fully describe either musical experience or human feeling states. Likewise, it is impossible to account for the human process of feeling attuned solely on the basis of which neurons might be firing, or which musical elements are being used. Wilburg suggests that 'tones of being' are shared wavelengths of *attunement* which connect us to our own being and at the same time link and join being with another. This seems to offer then a philosophical position on how listening deeply in music therapy might enable adopted people to experience attunement. To provide space wherein such attunement can occur means focusing on what might be going on for ourselves and our adopted clients internally ('tones of being'), as well as how we make sense of what is going on in the spaces between us ('tones of feeling') and in our relationality ('shared wavelengths of attunement' or intersubjectivity). It is the space between that intrigues me both as a musician and as a music therapist. Music comes into existence in the space between performer and audience, or between therapist and client. How do we create what we know as the therapeutic context in both time and space that means it is possible for what we identify as attuned music therapy to emerge? Becoming aware of our own embodied listening is crucial when working with adoptees who missed those earliest times of making communicative relational sounds and gestures that were not met in the birth mother's listening embodied being.

The known therapeutic effects of music underpinning the basic premise of music therapy

As a psychoanalytically informed music therapist, I believe music may express emotions, thoughts and unconscious states and conflicts that are not accessible with words. This is the basic premise of why we might use music therapy in adoption – because it offers a purchase on early pre-linguistic experience. Music has unique properties that we sometimes might be required to explain in order to argue why the 'therapeutic effects' of music might 'work' with our clients. Sami Alanne (2016, p.10) states, 'Music holds complex feelings as a conscious mastering of mind, and provides words to describe emotions.' This statement offers both an explanation for music's effects, and reasons as to why music is a useful modality for working with adoptees. Where early life experiences and especially trauma have impacted the internal world of the child, music can provide a language of expression. The remainder of this chapter will set out some of the philosophical basis of why it might be that what I am doing clinically with music therapy with adoptees is 'working'.

Music as a language for emotions and unconscious states

Music can help us to do psychic work with an individual because it provides a symbolic language and symbolic distancing from traumatic experience. Music can become perhaps, in Winnicott's terms (1971), a transitional phenomenon or an object. Alanne tells us it 'can create feelings of safety while one is suffering' (2016, p.11).

There is debate among music therapists about whether music exists as a language or a dynamic form, and our profession contains widely differing perspectives on this. Developmental psychology suggests that musical experience is rooted in the proto-conversations between a mother and baby (Stern). Music can be thought of as pre-language, or early babbling, and vocalizations (described as 'motherese' by Stern) can be seen as musical in themselves. Stern's infant observations were couched in a very musical language that has permeated music therapy language. Can we imply perhaps that music precedes symbolic spoken language as a sort of 'pre-language'? Might music even be described as the 'first language' for at least some children (as suggested to me by the music therapist Karen Gold, 2016)?

Music and brain science

Alanne (2016) cites the period 2000–2009 as a time when much new thinking about music and the brain was published, and consequently there is a wealth of writing about music and brain science accessible to music therapists. Interest has increased in understanding ways in which music is processed and experienced. Also, this period saw a huge output of research and publishing about trauma and the brain. The basic premise that early trauma impacts on brain development is now discussed even in popular media and accepted as 'fact'. Secure attachment is shown to affect the social brain, and therefore 'failed' attachments (including those lost in the process of adoption itself, without any additional trauma, and others lost when adoption is complicated by additional traumatic experience) can lead to epigenetic changes. One of the most recognized of such changes is a poor capability for affect regulation. Music can create potential wellbeing in the brain, and therefore may have an evolutionary importance in creating secure attachments (Siegel and Solomon 2013).

Recent discovery of the significance of mirror neurons in the human brain suggests that 'mirroring' is essential as only in such shared being is a more direct access to intentional states of others available (Siegel and Solomon 2013). Knox (2011) states that the observation and imitation of the expression of emotions not only activates the same expressions in the music therapist but also the same group of brain structures, a mirror-matching mechanism. This enables us to recognize intent in others' emotions. The mirror neuron system automatically prompts the observer to resonate with the emotional state of another individual and is the basis of the experience of 'emotional contagion', or 'feeling with' or, in Wilburg's language, sharing 'tones of feeling'. Matching and mirroring have long been recognized as basic core music therapy techniques. Learning about mirror neurons aids our understanding of the significance of how human beings jointly share impulses, such as those we call rhythms and harmonies. However, this neurobiology further informs us that it is not the application of technique that is significant when we seek to consciously musically match and mirror. Rather, it is the felt experience that is the referent. Therefore, the sharing of felt musical experiences via mirror neurons might partially explain why music 'works' and has such potential for relational work at the deepest level – and is especially useful in adoption.

Rose (2004) additionally describes how music affects the same brain systems that trauma has affected. This extra piece in the 'jigsaw' lends weight to the suggestion that music might be a preferred modality to aid reparation of neural pathways which have been curtailed by traumatic experience (the neuroscience of trauma has been well described in the work of Rothschild 2000, Van der Kolk 2014 and many others). The first memories for a baby are not recalled verbally but rather are sensed in 'amodal feelings' embodied in the self (Sletvold 2014). These are ambient experiences which form mutual affect attunement, internalized from the mother-infant dyad. Rose proposes that musical knowing and experiencing are equal to this embodied language of early life, giving further weight to why music therapy has potential for working with early lived experience.

Music therapists listening as an embodied holding process

In verbal language, we might refer symbolically to 'holding' someone in our gaze. This symbolic description of an aspect of human relating draws on a very real felt sense of the significance of gaze and eye contact that therapists know is so important in early life. Schore (1994) demonstrates how gaze plays a crucial part in the development of a sense of self and of other and underpins all relating that develops out of the earliest relationship. I suggest that as music therapists we can also 'hold' someone symbolically in our *listening*, which might be termed a sort of 'aural gaze'. Wilburg suggests 'our listening bodies...are in touch vibrationally' (2013, p.45), but he is describing language interactions specifically, and talks about how sensitive adjustment of language and tone of voice helps to modulate the holding. I suggest that music therapists similarly adjust dynamics, tempo, tonal qualities and so on, as we provide a 'holding musical gaze'. Musical holding is something explored in detail in Chapter 3, drawing on Winnicott's work. Winnicott says holding happens when we convey 'at the appropriate moment something that shows that (the analyst) knows and understands the deepest anxiety that is being experienced' (cited in Wilburg 2013, p.63). Might this sensitivity in the moment be something that happens both in playing and in our embodied listening which communicates to our clients that they are both heard and held?

Playing music together with adopted children

When we engage in playing and listening with an adopted child, we are fundamentally setting up relationships and learning about how that adoptee has previously experienced relationships. There is a danger (especially when we are newly qualified) for music therapists to view any music our client plays as a positive sign of their healthy relating. Yet adopted children can often engage in music-making that is anything but relational or signifying emotional health. The early music-making of adopted children in sessions may resist any joining, and be defensive, or it may be overly compliant. Vulnerable adopted children who fear further rejection might ask us to tell them which instrument we want them to play and how to play it (see Chapter 3). The purpose of music therapy for adoptees is not about making their own music, separate from relating, nor is it to make compliant music; the purpose is helping an adoptee to access an authentic playing self in relationship. The function of both defensive and compliant playing is interesting to think about as it features so often in work with adoptees.

The effects of a loss of maternal holding (in the Winnicottian sense) are evident musically with many adopted clients. For some, this loss has come in the form of a very early separation from a birth mother when they may have been even minutes old. Others who have had longer time with their birth mother may not have had a good experience of being held. A birth mother who is herself depressed or otherwise stressed (not least because she is losing her baby) may not be present enough for her baby and therefore unable to provide that sense of being. Adoptees removed because their birth mothers were misusing drugs, which left them exposed to huge unreliability, have early encounters with the world that are experienced as discontinuous surges. Children who additionally experienced the trauma of emotional, physical and psychological abuse are impinged on in the extreme. A baby is utterly unable to respond to these experiences other than in embodied states. They may learn quickly that defence and compliance are best.

How then might music therapy offer children access to their authentic playing self? Client-led improvisations are essential so that authenticity is not constrained by a music therapist dictating what or how to play. Music therapists need to constantly monitor their own 'tones of being' to receive the client's 'tones of feeling'. Are we able to allow for free responses, or do we move too quickly and react? Frustrated by a child's unwillingness to engage might we react prematurely with attempts at musical mirroring and matching that are not emotionally embodied? Can we find ways to play ourselves that allow adopted children space to enjoy experimenting with the available sound world, while ensuring they feel held enough to risk doing so? How do we avoid the danger of offering too little, which might leave the child feeling musically 'abandoned', or too much, which might mean they feel musically 'interfered with'? (See Chapter 3 for a description of the continuum of interference and abandonment.)

Specific musical features in adoption work: holding an aural gaze in rhythm and repetition

The adoptee's body as it engages in embodied acts of playing music can reveal unconscious states within music therapy, but there is also much that the music that is being created itself can reveal. As music therapists, our embodied listening means we take in the emotional feeling tones of our client, *and* we simultaneously listen to and interact with the musical forms being produced, considering their impact. We listen in the music to the tonality, the melody (or lack thereof), the rhythm and pulse, the tempo, the dynamic and so on. Certain musical features are regularly apparent in my work with adopted children and I will now describe these.

Rhythm

Rhythm is core to a sense of self (Stern 2010). We begin our existence in rhythm, from the time of conception, through hearing the rhythms of our mother's voice in utero, and then on entering the world. Our first in-breath sets up a rhythm, echoed in our first cry and out-breath. Therapists who have written about early mother-infant communications identify rhythm as one of the major factors of relationship. The mother-infant relationship is characterized by attention to movement, rhythm, timing and micro-moment emotional interaction, which is a focus Stern (2010) terms forms of vitality (2010).

Children removed from their birth mother experience an enormous disruption to their fundamental life rhythm. The unifying pulse is broken, and the baby has to attempt to learn a new tempo. When adopted children first come to music therapy, I've found their rhythmic relating is consistently difficult to connect to. Children will often play without any seeming sense of order or rhythmic coherence. Usually, the playing is flitting and fleeting, and chops and changes. Likewise, the instrument choice may be speedily changed (the instruments are often dropped or thrown or otherwise disregarded). When I try to join a rhythm that seems emergent, at the very moment a first rhythmic connection is felt, I simultaneously find the child has 'disappeared' rhythmically and I am somehow 'out of time' myself. (So consistent was the feeling of not being able to join in during the early days of my work that I wondered if I had somehow become unrhythmic!) However, I began to think instead that the adopted child does not initially want to be 'found' musically, or in fact does want to be found but is terrified of what this may mean (similar perhaps to Freud's 'Fort!' 'Da!' in that a distressing experience of something being lost is repeated, with the consequent need to be found, which is still yet perceived as frightening). Being musically found is a very visceral embodied experience. Sharing rhythm can feel like getting terrifyingly close for a child who fears attachment. Children who exist alone and independently in defensive music fear 'disappearing' if they risk sharing a rhythm with another, because it feels to them that it is only possible to exist independently.

In Chapter 8, case studies describe how the music therapy room after the first sessions has been described to me by parents as 'like a war zone'. Likewise, I can emerge from the music having a similar sense of having been attacked and destroyed. Bion's (1959) notion of 'attacks on linking' seems similar to what is happening here both literally and metaphorically in early music-making with adoptees. The minute a child feels relationally drawn close to in the music is the time they need to flee and break 'links' that suggest attachment. I have come to see this as a necessary aspect of the work which in some cases has to continue for months. First, it enables me to gain a sense of how fragmented the child has felt, and helps them to know that if they need to they can 'get away' from feelings that arise when connecting seems as if it might happen. Gradually then, as children know they will not be 'coerced' into play, we can begin to play embodied music together. When this happens for a child, there is frequently a sense of relinquishment, as finally they allow themselves to be 'found'. It may take years to reach this point, but it is usually evidenced by joy, smiles and laughter, with changes in song lyrics, and new delight in spontaneously mirrored embodied states. Winnicott (1965/1990) has the most beautiful description of what this experience is like:

> Here is a picture of a child establishing a private self that is not communicating and at the same time wanting to communicate and

to be found. It is a sophisticated game of hide-and-seek in which it is a joy to be hidden but disaster not to be found (p.187).

Repetition, chord circling, ostinato

Rhythm and repetition go together. For a rhythm to feel rhythmic, it will have to be repeated. Repetition is another feature that adopted children seem to crave in their music-making. I became aware quite early on in the work that repeating rhythmic patterns had a stabilizing and holding quality that children were adept at seeking out. Children preferred melodies that were played over repeated chords, and often the fewer chords the better. Robarts (2014) has described well the sort of music that needs to be created; 'banal in its predictability, wherein lies its therapeutic value' (p.76). Sometimes we might together invent a song with just two chords, the accompaniment rocking between perhaps a C and a G chord, usually using the root and fifth so as not to give the music any pre-conceived tonality, leaving both major and minor options open. Such music is incredibly simple (and even, I admit to agreeing with Robarts, boring or banal for a musician! See Chapter 3), yet bears similarity to the constant repetitive holding and rocking a baby needs (and the inevitable boredom a parent sometimes feels!). Older children have chosen to improvise themselves playing with a circling chord pattern; one of the most obvious (and found in a lot of contemporary pop) is C-Amin-F-G. This pattern raises expectation, creates a tension by slipping to the minor, brightens this with a return to a major, and resolves the cadence by the return from G to C (again, root and fifth). Many adopted children have improvised a wordless sung or instrumental melodic line for some minutes as I have offered the holding musical space of a circling chord pattern. Ostinato functions similarly. Music similar to Satie's 'Gymnopédies' has this holding quality, and also offers some sustenance in its rocking back and forth. If children have found ostinato helpful, I have suggested recorded music that they might share with parents at home, especially at times when they require emotional regulation. Improvising ostinato in sessions with a child can create a place of stillness to engender emotional equilibrium. In sessions, children can lie down, perhaps with a blanket or toy, as I provide ostinato improvisation myself as a way of sustaining a facilitative and holding environment.

Specifically, then, what I believe music therapy is offering within adoption is first a place for deep embodied listening, wherein a child might feel held in an 'aural gaze'. Once this is established, the ground is paved for possibilities for intersubjective relating (to be discussed more in Chapter 9). My understanding of intersubjectivity as it occurs within music therapy is that it is the embodied relational matrix out of which each individual human being both emerges and in which he or she also remains embedded. This embodied relational matrix will be evident in the music and the relationship that evolve. The attachment communications and music of adopted children, as we have seen, are expressed at levels beneath conscious awareness within the dynamic intersubjective field. I have learned, then, to not reject any communication in the music therapy room but to think and reflect on possible meanings. Music therapy becomes a language for affect-laden material, in work that attempts to make unconscious but embodied relational experience more conscious. The containing and holding power of deep listening, or simply sitting beside a child and humming a soft melody, provides an attending, waiting, reflecting space of shared observed attention wherein the child can experience themselves and their thoughts and feelings in the 'now' moment (Stern). Hearing themselves reflected in a musical relationship gives a vital sense to these children of being alive in the presence of another, a sense that was lost from their first attachment possibility with their birth mother. Knox (2011) describes this as 'witnessing' (which is further discussed in Chapter 7), and such necessary reflecting back of the affective state of a child is groundwork for the safe contained expression of trauma. Tuning in to all aspects of music, including the embodied but unsounded music of an adopted child's internal world, can offer a new experience of relating that might engender a process of relational reparation that continues outside the therapy room. In this way, there is hope that lives and placements can be renewed.

Chapter 7

How Music Therapy Supports Adoptions in Difficulty

We have so far explored some of the contexts that shape contemporary adoption – historical, social, cultural, and political – and the contemporary processes leading to the placements of children we are likely to work with. This chapter now draws in the lens to focus on the familial. What happens in adopted families that leads to them seeking additional professional support, and either requesting music therapy for themselves or being referred to music therapy by another agency? How is music therapy understood and perceived within the adoption community as being of potential value and help? How has it been constructed within the ideology that undergirds the establishment of the Adoption Support Fund (so that music therapy is now a recognized provision that the ASF will provide funding for)? What approach might music therapists take to address complex adoption referrals?

As discussed in Chapter 4, the majority of music therapy referrals now come direct from families (or their adoption support workers) in the midst of dealing with manifest difficulties (as described in Chapters 1 and 2), and some who, in extremis, are facing adoption placement disruption and breakdown. A few referrals may be made in the early days of a placement when it is anticipated that extra support might be required (such as in the placements of children with additional special needs, with complex trauma and in sibling groups).

Families as self-referrers

The establishment of the Adoption Support Fund (ASF) in 2015 meant families themselves could access therapeutic support for their children. This has been enormously empowering for parents within the adoption community. Previously they would have had to go to the child's placing social work team to request therapy, and would have had to compete for very limited resources. However, there are potential issues when adoptive parents are responsible for referral criteria for accessing music (and other) therapies. Referral may be constructed by the parents' perceptions of the difficulties either they believe their children are experiencing, or that they as adoptive parents are experiencing with their children. Children themselves may not be aware of any 'problem' existing (such as attachment disorder that may be viewed as residing within themselves, or any other difficulty related to their pre-adoption experience). As many children have no conscious recollection of their early life, or are troubled by current difficulties, they may not see any need to attend therapy and justly resist being pathologized.

Since 2015, varying stories have emerged of families who access the ASF. Parents who approach the ASF for support have often attempted to get help via other means and may even have had previous experiences of therapy which may or may not have been adoption, attachment and trauma informed. Parents report their children resisting verbal therapy because they don't know what to say when they are asked to talk about adoption. Some children internally already feel a sense that they are somehow inherently 'bad' and that this is why their birth parents gave them away. Such children risk being made to feel validated in their perception that 'something is wrong' with them, or that they are 'damaged goods'. Children who were placed for adoption as very tiny babies are known to sometimes believe they must be really bad inside because they were too little to 'even have done anything wrong' to 'make' their parent give them up…so they must just have been a really horrible baby.

Many adoptive parents instigate their search for therapy because they feel their adopted children 'need' it because of difficulties they present. Children may be demonstrating 'behaviour difficulties' which may not be viewed through the lens of adoption/attachment.

This is especially true when older children may have not presented any challenge in placements over some years, but suddenly begin truanting, stealing, using drugs, abusing other children and so on. Often families return initially to the agency that placed the children (who they may have established ongoing contact with), or they might present at social services in a crisis situation (such as the threatened ending of an adoptive placement). At the point of requesting music therapy it may be the case in the adoptive parent's mind that the purpose is to do with 'sorting out' the behaviours presented. In this case, music therapy is identified as being solely for adoptees who carry the defined 'problem'.

Other families may present to health services, (such as at their local GP surgery) if a child is manifesting a difficulty that might be constructed as an issue for a health professional (such as concerns about mood disorder, eating disorder, psychosis). There may be concern and frustration around any emergent diagnostic disorder and, in the process of help-seeking, any thinking pertinent to adoption may not enter into the decision-making. Families who adopted their child as a baby and experienced no issues until perhaps the child's late teens may not feel there is any adoption-specific context that might help explain, for example, a teenage girl developing an eating disorder. Requests for therapeutic support, then, are often framed in contexts of manifest difficulties located solely within adopted children, and less so within the adoptive context itself. At the point of referral, it can require some work to enable families to risk exploring relational material that occurs between both adoptee and adopter, and to understand why an approach focused on relationship might be considered.

Thus, some children may come to music therapy under the guise of a referral pertaining to diagnosis, and only in the course of assessment might it transpire that a child is adopted. Some health authorities have adoption-specific CAMHS services, and children may gain access either to these, or to other CAMHS teams on the basis of which referral criteria are presented. Adoption-specific CAMHS will be able to think with the family about material related to adoption in the presence of additional diagnosis; however, families report that accessing such teams is extremely difficult, and referral 'gatekeeping' means only severe mental health presentations are accepted.

Many families will already be familiar with the formal diagnosis of 'attachment disorder' which is usually discussed in preparation groups for adopters. They may therefore have concerns that the difficulties their children are experiencing might constitute such a disorder. As discussed in Chapter 2, traditional parenting skills need adapting to 'therapeutic parenting' (Cairnes 2002) if adopters are going to meet the needs of children described as having attachment disorder, yet often families will state that even therapeutic parenting is failing. Certainly, traumatic experiences do alter the neurological functioning of adopted children, and those who have experienced extreme abuse and neglect do struggle to attune emotionally to even the most skilled and sensitive adoptive parents. Adopters in turn present with varying degrees of empathy regarding the trauma their children have experienced, and how this may re-present.

Reframing the referral

It can be more difficult for adoptive parents to understand how children are managing trauma that is perceived as less extreme. The neuroscience about the development of the brain being dependent on emotional experience is becoming more mainstream and accessible if parents want to learn more. Many parents will be keen to learn how their children will have absorbed overwhelming sensations of abandonment, even as tiny babies, and how this can have enduring effects. Parents I have worked with have found quite complicated information easier to grasp when explained in a narrative form, and Verrier's (1993) book, *The Primal Wound*, is a text that does this. Writing such as this gives parents a purchase on the impact of early life material in a way that makes sense. Sharing such texts can be an essential part of the early stages of therapy, supported by the team around the music therapist.

I first discovered the Welsh word 'hiraeth', meaning 'homesickness tinged with grief over loss and a yearning for a place to which you cannot return' when a family I was working with stated that this was the feeling they imagined their child was struggling with. It encapsulates beautifully the sense that might dominate an adopted child's feelings, and other families have similarly been encouraged to imagine such loss and yearning. More mystifying, however, is the fact that an adopted child will never actually have really known that place of being in a birth family, but instead will have almost certainly developed fantasies fuelled by social narratives about what a 'real family' is. Winterson's (2011) autobiography referred to in Chapter 2 is another text that provides description of the power of such feelings and can be useful reading for parents struggling to understand their children's difficulties. Winterson herself could not make sense of the immense mental health difficulties that seemed to suddenly beset her in mid-life, but as she embarked on therapy she was enabled to locate her emotional crisis back in her experience of abandonment as a baby.

Some families do, however, come easily to a view that any particular symptomatic or behavioural issues could perhaps be related to a child being adopted, and a manifestation of a struggle to manage unconscious material from their pre-placement life.

Explaining and understanding adoption trauma and its impact

What we can now be sure of is that adopted children carry internalized knowledge of their early trauma, however early it was. They know in their deepest cell memory what has happened to them. Older children who are placed may of course have very real live memories of earlier traumatic lived experience. They may have experienced emotional, physical and sexual abuse at a developmental level where they had language to describe what was happening, and indeed where such descriptions/disclosures may have resulted in removal. Other children may have been born with disabilities that their parent was unable to deal with because they themselves had learning difficulties sufficient to impact on their parenting ability.

All of these earlier lived experiences will undoubtedly become evident in music therapy in what Margaret Wilkinson (2010) describes as 'the old present'. As discussed earlier in this book, by this Wilkinson means that early/old experiences are remembered and form aspects of a child's internal world, and therefore the old becomes present and alive when it is re-enacted in new relationships. Almost all the children I have worked with in music therapy have at some point acted out play involving 'ghosts' (as has been described also by Robarts 2014, and detailed further in Chapter 8 of this book). Ghosts might describe difficult early experiences that remain buried within, unknown and unknowable to the child but available as a feeling. Chapter 1 stated how strong emotions of distressing events are stored principally in the amygdala, unavailable to recall, yet governing ways of being and behaving. Neurobiology has transformed our understanding of what it means to 'remember' trauma by demonstrating what happens when a memory is evoked. Areas of the brain dedicated to verbal and autobiographical memory are inhibited while structures in non-verbal areas become highly active, showing increased emotional, perceptual and body memories.

Because of this, the pre-symbolic/pre-conscious level at which we experience music in the body as emotion has a special role in work with adoption. Adopted children can find safety in improvised music, trusting their own phrasing and patterns, feeling grounded in their own music, while processing and assimilating the emotional impact of traumatic experience in musical relating with their music therapist. Indeed, Chapter 1 suggested that the prosodic interchanges in music therapy seem to emanate from the proto-conversation of mother and baby. From as early as 18 weeks' gestation the foetus knows the intonation and timbre of mother's voice (Gallese 2005) and this is the basis of prenatal attachment through sound, having significance in respect to its emotional quality, relational engagement, interaction and loving affection. When children are enabled to play in attuned ways, early intuitive emotional communication becomes evident in dynamic form (Trevarthen 1979), or 'communicative musicality'. Sutton (2002) succinctly describes the potential value of music therapy for trauma survivors (and therefore I suggest for adoptees) because it offers 'experiences of ourselves as embodied in sound and in silence' (p.35). Later in this chapter we will think more about why this may be of particular significance given what adopted children might need from therapy.

Framing the arts therapies as modalities for adoption work

There is little common ground of experience, then, for deciding what sorts of therapeutic help might be most useful to families that show such diversity of presentation at referral. However, all of the creative arts therapies are recognized by the ASF and are defined as 'therapeutic services not currently provided by local authorities'. For any music therapist to have credence with the ASF and with their local authority, it is imperative that they have developed and received additional training in adoption and attachment-informed work. Such a knowledge base and experience are necessary if a therapist is going to be able to help both children and parents manage and accommodate the distinctiveness of adoption experience as a chosen form for permanent family life. However, both families and social workers may not have a lot of knowledge or information about therapeutic modalities, nor understand why they might 'work'. Therefore, it is incumbent on us as music therapists to offer explanations to those seeking therapy, and to provide concise descriptions about what a non-verbal modality might provide and why music therapy is specially placed to work with pre-linguistic trauma. The free leaflet describing music therapy in adoption that is available on the British Association for Music Therapy website can be offered to both adoption professionals and families as it succinctly describes how music therapy might help with adoption-related issues (see Appendix 2).

Why, then, is music therapy considered to be a therapeutic modality of choice for adoption, and how do we explain this? It is possible to describe to adoptive parents, in the languages of both attachment and music, why music therapy has something special to offer to adoptees. First, we can identify that music possesses specific aspects and qualities such as rhythm, timing, intensity and dissonance, which are the same qualities described in literature pertaining to early life relating (Trevarthen 1979; Stern 1985; Beebe and Lachmann 2002; Tronick 2007). As the music therapist Robarts (2014) states, 'Musical expression directly engages and activates the core of rhythmic and sympathetic impulses from which all human communication comes' (p.71). These qualities also are described in relational embodied psychotherapy as being reparative aspects in therapy. By playing and listening to music together, a child and music therapist are inevitably involved in embodied relational work and can learn further about how to develop these aspects of music therapy. Stern's (2004) language has a natural musicality to it, when he writes of rhythms of relating and so on, and this can be made accessible to parents.

We can also explain simply to families how co-created, improvisational music-making can contain all the elements of attachment formation. A music therapy relationship that is naturally embodied can first of all help us to gain an understanding of an individual child's (and parent's, if working with dyads) internal worlds, which then can enable us to work with traumatic material from their early life that is impinging on the here-and-now relating within adoptive placements.

In Chapter 1, I introduced Stern's work on intersubjectivity, and his concept of affect attunement. The music therapist can share his theory quite simply with families by describing that when this felt sense is missed out on, it can impair intersubjective relating, because a baby loses their core source of rhythmic and sympathetic impulses. This in turn affects their developing brain connectivity, self-regulation and attachment capacity. Adoptive parents can be enabled to see how the attunement part of relating is missing between any birth mother and child who did not have those precious few hours, days and weeks of relating. Then the music therapist can describe how the music therapy relationship and setting provide a creative, safe space for possibilities for new attuned relating to happen. The apparent simplicity of the therapeutic frame in its regularity of time and place is a rhythmic structure in itself. However, because attunement is a spontaneous happening, we must clarify that we cannot prescribe it happening, nor create a model of how it might happen. This is why each child should be engaged with in a needs-led way, and why the spontaneity of musical improvisations is so useful, and perhaps akin to the 'sloppiness' or 'intentional fuzziness' that Stern (2004) values. There is a lack of certainty and clarity which often might characterize adoption music therapy, but there are parameters we can establish in order for there to be a space created in which it might occur.

The distinct nature of adoption work

All children who are removed from their birth families will have experienced attunement-related losses, and both fostering and adoption have enough in common to formulate some core guiding principles and music therapy practice for both. However, adoption is distinctive in that it is a permanent placement for a child and as such offers the necessary stability for therapy to be safely embarked on. From the minute an adoption order is made, children become legally the children of their adopters, who have all legal rights exactly as if they were birth parents. From this point, the family will not experience regular reviews, for example, which are a feature of even long-term fostering. It is this definite permanency which underlay my own choice to work solely within adoption, as children are unlikely to be subject to moves, and risk losing contact with therapy, thereby experiencing another attachment loss. Even when an adoption placement is undergoing severe stress and there is talk of possible placement breakdown, the children still have a legal and permanent defined relationship with their adopters, and it is this which therapy might aim to preserve. It is also necessary for children to have this degree of permanency if they are going to commit to work that will raise early life material, creating vulnerability and dependence (often via regressive states). Parents also need to be committed and adequately supported to staying the course when things get worse before getting better.

'But it's not my problem!' When children are referred as the locus of a presenting problem, but issues lie within relational dynamics

I have described how when an adoptive family seek help, it is the child who is frequently presented as having a 'problem'. There usually needs to be preparatory work with families before the start of music therapy that can enable them to understand the relational nature of attachment, and how therefore the help for attachment difficulties also needs to be relational. For parents, the desire to believe in answers and cures for adopted children's presentations, and to come up with tidy formulations of difficulties can be strong. However, when certainty of this sort is neither helpful nor possible, we need as music therapists to instead find ways and develop therapeutic styles of sense-making for any presenting issues, symptoms, behaviours and experiences.

My own approach involves first explaining to parents that their children cannot be 'fixed' simply if the right tools or techniques are used. Sometimes, in hearing of this lack of a fix or cure, all parties are enabled again to face the losses accrued in adoption, and the sadness that this leads to which may be expressed in behavioural presentations. I explain to families that we endeavour to engage adopted children in music therapy that does not focus on a diagnostic label but rather on the context within which such a diagnosis might have occurred and been construed. When families ask how music therapy 'works', it is possible to describe how we provide time and space to play in, which the child lost in early life. Parental empathy can be re-ignited when they recall all that their child has lost and experienced (for example, if the child was abused prior to placement). This leads to explanations of the value of needs-led improvisational music-making, and again parents can be offered explanation of how and why this can be helpful for the child. Parents and other referrers may initially hope that therapy is somehow going to do something to the child that will change them, and we need to become skilled at explaining how improvisation might reveal unconscious relational patterns from a child's inner world. Only by providing space for children to reveal themselves might we – parents, referrer and music therapist alike – be able together to make sense of what is revealed.

What can be more difficult to explain to parents are issues that their child might have in relating to them because of the interplay of internal worlds. It can sometimes seem to parents that any blame for the difficulties they present with is being shifted from the child and back on to them. This is why families might describe previous engagements with therapy as feeling pathologizing. As music therapists, we need to be alive to explaining that these difficulties happen in the spaces between people, and we don't seek to locate damage in individuals. It can mean that we need to draw on the team around us to provide support and education for parents in the dynamics of attachment in placements. Some adopted children are uncannily aware of the expectations their adopters carry, which linger on from fantasies about the birth children their adopters never had. Children might unconsciously protect their adoptive parents from the death of these fantasies by trying hard to become the fantasy child. They may also attempt to be anything but the fantasy child, feeling that any birth child would be the ultimate competitor for the parents' affections and attention. Adopted children who have been able to verbalize their feelings have indicated that they felt they needed to keep their adopters' fantasies alive, and could not risk being 'real' themselves, because they could not believe their reality was wanted.

Such children are extremely sensitive to any response from their therapist that may suggest the therapist feels they are somehow the site of damage. Great care needs to be taken with both children and parents to ensure we offer a safe space to relate authentically, without fear of blame and judgement. This is also why the processes of the adoption panel (see Chapter 4) that led to the placement are helpful to know. Parents will have had to present themselves over and over as being good enough to adopt, and children will know that they can be chosen or rejected. These processes can impact on future relating with professionals, and certainly can affect the ways that music therapy is thought about and experienced.

CASE VIGNETTE: **KEVIN**, **PAULINE** AND **FREDDIE**

Kevin and Pauline sought music therapy for Freddie, aged two. Freddie was having tantrums around bedtime routines. Kevin and Pauline thought that by the age of two Freddie should be taken off to bed and settled so they could have the evening being quiet together. Instead, Freddie was increasingly disruptive, causing chaos at bath time, then refusing to go to his room, which he would proceed to 'destroy'. Kevin was extremely angry with Freddie, who he had begun to view as a competitor for Pauline's time. Pauline felt like a failure as she had always imagined idyllic bedtimes with her child. Freddie was engendering a dynamic of splitting in the couple, which was resonant of his early life experiences in his birth family. To embark on music therapy, the family needed time to express their fantasies and losses so they could engage with the very real needs of a real little boy, who could not bear separation from his mother.

Realities and difficulties of working with lived experience and sense-making: becoming a 'silent witness'

When we attempt to work with the lived experience of adoptees, we soon learn that we cannot 'fix' things for either child or family, and that painful and distressing events have occurred for all involved, impacting at a deep relational level. An approach that is needs-led can feel destabilizing for the music therapist. We can fear seeming incompetent as we gently explore and begin to shape any sense of what is happening to and for a child and family, but without a goal or plan. It is important that both child and family are continuously involved in co-constructing sense-making about what their lived experience has meant and how surviving difficult experience has required differing mechanisms. The journey of anyone's music therapy is always a very uncertain one, for both client and therapist, as we can never be sure of what lies ahead, nor how the journey might end, and yet can be pressed for such certainties either from the family, or by other professionals. Love (2007) writes about the need for therapists to live with our clients' experience of 'injury', without fixing it. Glassman and Botticelli (2014, p.175) write:

> to a therapist's ear, such quiet acceptance of clients' circumstances jangles, grating against our therapeutic ambitions, our will to repair, and wishes for our patients (and our own) progress. Yet with some people it may be all we can do, all we're allowed to do, to be a witness to injury.

There is, however, immense value in first offering a witnessing stance.

Witnessing

A witnessing stance might sit uncomfortably if we are asked to offer a music therapy that can define 'aims and objectives' or delineate at the start what an 'outcome measure' should be for a client. These pressures must be declined, however, when we work genuinely in client-led ways, and with the lived experience of the adoption community. Glassman and Botticelli state that therapists working in such a way have to present their work 'as a testament to the complex and deeply personal purposes to which our patients may put us, *purposes undreamt of in the mind of the evidence-based treatment researcher*' (2014, p.175; emphasis added). It is often the case that the pressures are released somewhat when working with adoptions in crisis because families will already have run the gauntlet of available interventions, and there can be sheer desperation for anything that might prevent an adoption breaking down. However, we cannot state that preventing adoption breakdown even is our aim, because this can never be guaranteed and also because some adoptions may not be good for anyone involved and may need to break down.

In a client-led way of working that draws on lived experiences, each client will inevitably help us to shape what sort of music therapy we offer as, essentially, we come alongside the client on what is actually their journey. In early sessions, as we predominantly witness client narratives, we offer what seems simply described as a supportive presence. This may mean that not a lot of music gets played, and that as music therapist we are cast in the role of listener. This is not nearly as easy to provide as it might sound.

CASE VIGNETTE: **FREDDIE**

Freddie was described as loving music and he did seem very excited when he visited the music room and saw all the instruments available. However, when he came to music therapy, he found a place to sit on the floor, and instead of attempting to play any instrument, he gathered them around him and proceeded to make a pretend fortress with them. Any supportive playing that the therapist offered was met with Freddie shrieking and running to remove her hands from the keyboard. For some weeks, Freddie built his fortress as the therapist sat silently witnessing and listening. She was able to share with Kevin and Pauline how terrified Freddie was of becoming close to anyone, and describe the towers he built for his protection.

Gradually, in working together we hope that a jointly evolved sense of meaning arises between the client/family and therapist. But even this cannot be guaranteed. At times, there may be aspects of this meaning-making that are verbalized. In my practice, either I, or others in the team, may offer theoretical material to adoptive parents that enables sense-making with them about why experiences that happened so early in life can continue to inform, influence and even dominate the present. At other times, the sense-making may be more implicit and not spoken about. The adopted client may share the sense I am making of things, or not, and I do not present my hypothesizing as the definitive last word on what might be going on. In this fluid relating between client, adoptive family and music therapist, new truths and new ways of relating may emerge, and they are just as likely to be new for the therapist as they are for the client.

Bjorkland (2014) likens this sense-making journey in therapy to the adoptees' broader search for meanings, and an organization of lived experience into coherent narrative form. She states that, 'sometimes the act of searching can be an act of freedom and agency that can enliven lost or disavowed selves. However, what we find may not be what we thought we were searching for' (p.82). This again reiterates why we cannot offer set outcomes for adoption work, as the outcome may be very different from what might be planned. Adopted children cannot know their early life experience, and only as this is revealed through relational play can anything of value be found.

This tentative gradual exploratory way of being sits well with the way free musical improvisation emerges. Heidegger (1959, p.44) states how 'in waiting, we leave open what we are waiting for'. He seems to be describing what I recognize happening in the music therapy room in client-led improvisation. An approach of open expectancy to the client, and indeed to improvisational music-making together, seems to be about this 'waiting' and witnessing. It is far from being inactive, however, and while we wait, our supportive witnessing presence is made available to the client through our silent listening or attuned, supportive, holding, containing playing. The apparent simplicity of offering musical waiting, witnessing and supporting is in fact an extremely complex process (further discussed in Chapter 6).

In these initial days of work with an adopted child, silence may dominate. In periods like this we may feel very clearly in transference how alone a client has been, and what they needed to do to care for themselves in order to survive. Babies and children learn automatic ways of surviving and coping, without any conscious connection to the events that conditioned them. Helping clients to notice and recognize their implicit memories as part of their adoption narrative is the first step in recovering from trauma. The client may choose silence for themselves, or may silence their therapist (as did Freddie). In my own practice, offering a musical witnessing might involve, for example, holding long, soft, sustained notes against which a client might improvise (as Austin 2009 mentions). The simplest long bows on my violin, or a sustained pedalled note on the piano, or vocally breathed out sounds soft and slow can provide enough of a sense of holding for the client to reveal their material. Our own musical contribution can seem even 'boring' as stated earlier. However, Eigen (2014) helpfully talks of 'boredom' being a necessary feature of therapy, and musically we might during such times be providing something which a child may be calling for from the deepest level. We are then profoundly alive and responsively attuned when we create this spontaneously and musically.

As music therapists, we can learn to trust our capacity to be with, witness, and bear the clients' suffering patiently, waiting. Providing witnessing presence is more about what we don't do than about any technique we use for 'doing'. It might not feel like a 'high point' of our sessions musically speaking, but it is a necessary gradual working through (perhaps not unlike 'going on being' in Winnicott's terms, or Stern's 'moving along' discussed in Chapter 2).

Benefits of the approach

To conclude this chapter, I shall describe some benefits of the sort of music therapy approach to diverse types of adoption referral described in this chapter. It is imperative that as music therapy practitioners we are able to understand the implications of the distinctiveness of the dynamics of adoption as a form of permanency and family life. Such understanding should underlie attempts to meet the adoption-specific needs that families and children present with.

As most therapy supported by the ASF is provided by freelance workers, we are usually able to offer prompt attention to clients who present seeking therapeutic help. Practice and research show that in many adoptions, crisis times will come, and that swift, careful, informed specialist attention can make the difference between placement breakdown or not (Fisher and Chamberlain 2000). When adoptive families engage in services such as CAMHS they are channelled into assessments where the aim is to establish diagnoses. Such assessment systems can delay actually commencing therapy with a family. Some families may deliberately avoid such a route, as adopters who have themselves been subject to enormous assessment when being approved may not relish professional scrutiny again. It has been suggested that adoption therapists develop a light assessment touch with imagination and creativity, and that this view is generally supported by adoptive parents (Hart and Lucock 2004).

Music therapists directly funded by the ASF are not attached to a particular team or restricted by a particular institutions protocol. We can therefore be flexible to a family's needs and even engage and re-engage with them over differing periods of time, as this is conducive to working with the lifelong adoption trajectory. Adoptive parents may feel that their parenting is coming under the spotlight, and this can make establishing a therapeutic relationship uniquely difficult. Having a relationship with a music therapist who is not allied to any agency, and who can continue in the relationship if necessary over years, can be extremely important to such families. Continuity of music therapist (in contrast to the uncertainty and multiple changes often seen in other professional services) can itself provide containment for the family.

The approach to referrals described in this chapter can avoid a symptoms-reduction or diagnosis-focused approach (though we may find that aspects of music therapy do obliquely result in, for example, the calming of a child's symptoms of anxiety, or a reduction of behavioural acting out). More broadly, we can have confidence in and talk about music therapy's unique elements which can enhance an adoptee's ability to regulate emotion and develop the capacity for reflective functioning. As music helps to soothe and calm behaviour, a safe space for thinking in can be created. Within this context, there is the possibility for new relational styles to begin to emerge and, it is hoped, for secure, fresh attachments to be risked.

Chapter 8

An Adoption Narrative Informing Music Therapy

This chapter illustrates all that has been presented and discussed so far as theory, philosophy and approach by drawing on examples from my own music therapy practice. I hope these narratives provide the best way for music therapists and other readers to engage in their own sense-making of the material discussed in earlier chapters, thus making theory more accessible to practice. All examples are composite cases. No single clinical case described is a total description of one single individual client. Rather, I combine various features of various clients thereby preserving anonymity, and I am grateful for those who have allowed their own stories to percolate these narratives.

I have chosen the examples in this chapter because I think they most clearly show what I would describe as the thematic concerns of adoption music therapy. Over the years I have been practising, I have noticed that time and again these themes emerge with adoptive families, and that particular metaphors resonate with the adoption situation. I suggest, then, that these particular concerns are part of the adoption-specific trajectory and how this manifests within the music therapy space.

As described in Chapters 1 and 2, potential placement breakdown has been a major reason that clients have been referred to therapy, and yet all potential breakdowns have to date been stabilized and the placements have continued. Therefore, discussion of my clinical work here can be reassuring for all creative arts therapists who may want to work within adoption, but who also might be worried about engaging in work where 'failure' seems likely or possible. Preventing breakdown has never been a 'goal' as this could put undue pressure on both the family and the therapist. However, by working in a needs-led way, and by witnessing and accepting the severity of the presenting issues and attendant risks, we can together with families find a way through.

The music of traumatized adopted children, especially at the beginning of therapeutic work, is neither tidy nor beautiful. We need to engage in all the mess and confusion that is brought to us. When we meet and contain messy spontaneous play and reflect it back musically, we can show a child that their distress is witnessed and held. Through its intrinsic sensory modality and psychophysiological effect, music can enable the development of a child's narrative of being, and within music an adopted child and therapist can play with new ways of being and relating. Music therapy provides a unique creative capacity to simulate and imitate the experience of the other and thereby provide as Freud (1922) stated a path that leads from identification by way of imitation to empathy. Within music therapy we can encompass adoptees' feelings in our embodied playing and listening states and express feeling tones in the music. Adoptees in turn can sense we empathize because they hear and feel this in our responses. As music therapists, we induce, in our embodied music, the emotional states prevailing in our clients, and make them tangible and conscious. Music therapy then becomes an essential element for the emergence of intersubjectivity, which can in turn lead to adoptees discovering new ways of relating within their adoptive families.

Starting at the very beginning

When placements are referred for therapy right at the beginning of an adoption placement, I work with parents and children together in the room, most usually with newly adoptive mothers and their children. Therapy with mother/child couples provides perhaps, in Winnicottian terms, a sense of safe supportive holding for the mother, so she can begin to hold and contain the 'baby' (or older child). Earlier chapters describe holding happening within the space that *both* music and relationship provide.

CASE VIGNETTE: **EDWARD**

Jenny, the adoptive mother of Edward, had previously been struggling with her own adoption history. She herself had been removed from her birth family as a very small baby, but knew little more about her beginnings. Jenny and her husband adopted Edward at the age of four; he had become a looked-after child after experiencing severe physical abuse from his birth parents. Jenny desperately wanted to care for Edward, but found her overtures consistently rejected by him. Overwhelmed by the pain and subsequent losses he had experienced, which echoed her own losses, she came to music therapy minimizing both. Her unconscious memory of early abandonment resulted in a style of parenting which was at the 'interference' end of the abandonment/interference continuum. She overloaded Edward sensorially by intruding into his play and becoming very bossy in the room, also trying to boss me and instruct me in what and how to play. It took considerable time for her to relax and allow music therapy to become a space where Edward could regress to very early states, and she could meet and mother him, making some reparation for the years lost to them. First, however, she needed to be enabled to hold her own internal baby; she had previously despised her younger self and needed to be brought into a new relationship with that little self. Only then could she meet Edward and enjoy moments that seemed like early reverie that they had not experienced as birth mother and child.

The gaze of a baby

Some children have to somehow manage to start from an even earlier place, as was the case for Andrew.

CASE VIGNETTE: **ANDREW**

For the first weeks of music therapy, Andrew did not play a note, and indeed barely moved. Instead, he sat at the keyboard, opposite me and facing me across the instrument, gazing directly into my eyes. When I shared video clips of Andrew with my supervisor, she thought the video was on pause, as the moments between us were so incredibly still. Yet, it felt necessary to be in this stillness with him. The theory of mirror neurons suggests that through such a shared 'being' state, Andrew might have been beginning to gain access to the existence and state of another. Knox (2011) states that this observation and imitation not only activates the same expressions in the music therapist but also the same group of brain structures – a mirror-matching mechanism. Chapter 6 details how the mirror neuron system automatically prompts the music therapist to resonate with the emotional state of the adoptee and is therefore the basis of an experience of 'emotional contagion', or 'feeling with'. Andrew had to experience my being with him before we could play together, and this is what Winnicott states about the earliest days and even moments of the mother-infant relationship – being precedes playing. Times of almost nothing going on between us are essential, especially for children who have experienced the worst sorts of intrusions in abuse. Gallese and Ammaniti (2013) emphasize the significance of stillness for micro-attunements. Our music, if there is any, may be a single sustaining note. As Sletvold states (2014, p.83), 'The embodied mind is the mind that is shaped by the feeling and sensing of our own, and other people's, moving bodies.' Andrew and I shared silent embodied states as a necessary base for playing together.

Ghosts from the past become present here and now: the old is present

In previous chapters, we have thought about how adopted children carry internalized knowledge of early trauma which can manifest in music therapy as 'the old present' (Wilkinson 2010). Almost all children I have worked with have at some point acted out play involving 'ghosts' (as described also by Robarts 2014). We know from earlier chapters how difficult early experiences are embodied, and that strong emotions remain principally stored in the amygdala, unavailable to recall, yet governing ways of being and behaving. Such experiences have often entered the music therapy room in the form of 'ghosts', as in Charmaine's case.

CASE VIGNETTE: **CHARMAINE**

Charmaine was seven when she began music therapy and she attended with her adopted mum. Charmaine was the only adopted child in a family where there were two birth children. She always knew she was adopted and felt that she was 'less than' her parents' birth children. (There is a high risk of breakdown for such placements, with sibling rivalry sometimes being potent between birth and adopted children.) Charmaine formed an immediate connection with the large gong, and played softly on it, creating real atmosphere and then gently creating layers and waves of sound in gradual crescendo, until the room felt full of vibrations. As she did this, I provided a consistent and enduring piano bass octave, rocking along in time with her gong-ing. There was a thickness to the quality of sound, or 'feeling tone', which felt very mysterious, as if a musical mist was surrounding all of us.

Suddenly Charmaine jumped backwards stating 'Did you see that?' and rushed to the opposite side of the gong to hide. Her mum and I said we hadn't seen anything. She shrugged and said, 'Maybe it was a ghost?' This play repeated over many weeks, with a build-up of a musically dense atmosphere, out of which things did seem to emerge, almost as shadows coming out of a mist. Charmaine continued to speak of ghosts, one day adding some xylophone playing, creating melodic support for her verbal narrative. I supported this on piano, continuing sustaining the bass octaves. Charmaine then began to sing of a 'ghost baby' that she could hear crying. Although the baby was never identified, Charmaine herself seemed very sad as she sang. This sad feeling tone needed acknowledgement and holding. After some weeks of being with the sadness, I instinctively felt my own music changing, as I began playing in 6/8 time, the classic rhythm of a lullaby. The music provided sound holding for both Charmaine and her adopter. Charmaine's body began to rock in time, as though the piano music was holding her sadness. As she rocked, I wondered about her internal baby, and that baby's longing for the birth mother. Perhaps that 'ghost baby' was musically held and could be comforted in this lullaby rhythm? Charmaine's embodied rocking enabled her to hold and soothe herself too, and embrace the abandoned little baby she had been. She longed to feel secure belonging to her adopted mother, but her 'ghost baby' painfully reminded her that mothers could abandon. We never spoke about this, but the symbolism seemed to do its work. In later sessions, Charmaine asked her adopted mum to wrap her in a blanket and hold her like a baby. They were re-creating moments of early life that had been lost to them. Throughout their enacting, I sustained the 6/8 lullaby, its repetition and rocking reminding me of the sense of a baby at the breast. New relating could now emerge.

Embodied affect-led music relating

Previous chapters have theoretically described how embodied states might express emotional affect, and how musical relationships, which occur in and through bodies playing instruments/singing, can express such emotions wordlessly. Embodied states, to be truly understood, need to be felt, and my work with ten-year-old Shayla certainly gave me this experience.

CASE VIGNETTE: **SHAYLA**

Shayla taught me about embodiment in an appropriately visceral way. She attended a special school for children on the autistic spectrum with low support needs, and was referred because staff felt her presentation was not consistent with her diagnosis. Shayla experienced daily outbursts of extreme distress and became inconsolable. In music therapy, Shayla, like Andrew (above), needed to sit and gaze. My supervisor wondered if there might be something of an attachment need expressed in her gazing. When I read Shayla's notes, it transpired that she was adopted, and prior to her adoption, there was a history of abuse and neglect, but her adoption status had gotten subsumed in the autism diagnosis. It was not known and thought about therefore in school, which understood her through a lens adjusted for autism, not attachment. Exploring transference feelings in response to her gaze, I realized I felt like an inadequate mother, unable to give or to do anything useful in music therapy, and this paralleled how her adopted mother felt too. One day, Shayla inadvertently knocked a beater off a xylophone, which made a single sound as it fell to the floor. Spontaneously, I took up the remaining beater and played a single note response. Shayla picked up the dropped beater...and played. We finally began a musical relationship. Shayla led music-making in this 'accidental' manner, always commencing with 'dropping' a beater. It was as if she continually revealed her enduring sense of being 'dropped' which could now be thought about safely in the music. Video recordings of sessions showed the 'dance' of attachment and attunement developing between us. I never consciously matched or mirrored my movements to hers, yet frequently symmetry existed between us. Music flowed out of embodied states that was intimate, close, matched and mirrored. Sletvold (2014, p.xvi) states, 'The ability to experience both similarities and differences between bodies constitutes the basis for the registration of significant affective experiences that emerge in a relationship. These registrations take place without the involvement of reflective thought or traditional forms of symbolic representation.' We never spoke directly of Shayla's early lived experience, but it was evident and could safely be enacted and considered.

Cross-modal attunement

Varying aspects of Stern's concept of attunement have been addressed earlier, but my next case example shows how music therapy can provide experiences of cross-modal attunement for an adopted child. This is an expressive matching, rather than an imitation, where each partner uses a different mode for expression (so, for example, a gesture might be matched with a vocal sound). The reference for the felt sense of attunement is the internal state and not the external behavioural act.

CASE VIGNETTE: **LESLEY**

Lesley was at a stage in music therapy where she needed to exert control, deciding when I was 'allowed' to play. Gentle attempts I made to join her playing were met with bursts of outrage, screaming and crying. After some repeated experience of this, I also made a very loud (but non-aggressive, enduring and sustaining) vocalization, matching hers in terms of both volume and intensity. At the same time, I raised my arms in an enormous gesture, simultaneously opening my eyes very wide. In this cross-modal attunement, vocal cries were met in expansive embodied gestures. Initially astonished, Lesley then giggled, and I sensed she felt an embodied reciprocity, soothing distress from her experience, making it more safely tangible and shareable. Her states were not denied, but embraced, and such acceptance provided relational space for her to change something. We became able gradually to turn our vocalizations and gestures into songs, to which Lesley added drumbeats, eventually allowing me to join in on piano. She required an intensity of meeting to match and transform her own states, and thus eventually, through singing and playing together, rage was transformed into something more bearable.

Stern describes cross-modal rhythms, such as a baby giggling and a mother matching the rhythm with a body movement. This is how the emergence of discrete feeling states such as happiness, anger and fear might be shared. 'Vitality affects' or forms of vitality are the ever-changing feeling shapes, reflecting the intensity, strength and rapidity of interactions. Stern (2010, p.96) explains:

> They are the felt experience of force – in movement – with a temporal contour and a sense of aliveness, going somewhere. They do not belong to any particular content. They are more form than content. They concern the How, the manner and the style, not the What or the Why.

Such vitality affects were experienced in the manner and style of the flow of becoming attuned with Lesley.

Gaining emotional regulation

CASE VIGNETTE: **KEVIN**

Four-year-old Kevin was fairly new in placement with his single-carer mum, who had herself grown up in the care system. Music therapy happened as a parent-child dyad as his adopted mum had expressed an inability to attach to Kevin. She thought this was due to his pre-adoption experiences of physical abuse, which resonated with her own. In the room, Kevin moved rapidly and noisily, bashing, banging and often inadvertently damaging instruments in the process. As I was desperately wondering how to provide containment, Kevin's mum would be encouraging him to do yet more and more, her own voice becoming high pitched, rapid and over excited. In the transference, I felt as if I had two children who were impossible to hold onto in the room. Each time I found a thought arising in my mind to possibly interject into the situation, I would hear mum speaking: 'Show the music lady...show her the song you learned at school...show her how you play piano...show her your shoes...show her your school book...' and so on.

Supervision helped me realize that attempts to work verbally with Kevin's mum's verbal material were failing as she could never allow space. Rather than matching and mirroring the intensity, I instead offered a very different embodied presence in the room as a means of emotional regulation. I sat on the floor gently playing soft, almost inaudible, glissandos on a child's xylophone. This felt hopeless, in the face of the noise and chaos around me, and supervision identified that my feeling state might be like Kevin's, who also could not 'get a word in edgeways' and whose 'vitality effects' in the room might arise from a desire to please his mum. Gradually, Kevin began to hear the xylophone. In a rare moment's silence, he listened and was stilled. I found myself say, 'Perhaps Kevin and mum can just do nothing here if they want?'. Kevin sat down on a sofa, drawing a blanket around himself. Mum followed, at first discouraging him as she thought he would go to sleep, but gradually relenting and sitting alongside him. As the xylophone continued soft glissandos, Kevin lay down, placing his head in his mum's lap. He could not see her face, but her eyes filled with tears. As I continued to play, she began to stroke his hair. (Only later, watching the video, did I become aware that she and I shared an exact timing of movement, me in my xylophone glissando and she in hair stroking.) Kevin picked up a beater and made the softest of sounds on my xylophone. This emerged into a version of 'Twinkle Twinkle Little Star' (picked up by me melodically from a rhythmic figure he had begun). The three of us sat; mum stroking Kevin's hair, me playing, and Kevin snuggling into his mum while half playing. Kevin could safely regress, allowing the nursery song that we played together, along with the regular rhythmic sensorial stroking of his head by his mum, to provide some emotional regulation.

After this session, I met with his mum alone. She told me how her own traumatic memories of physical abuse were being evoked by Kevin. Her trauma had to be defended against, and so all potential space in the room was filled with what she described as 'noise' and 'fun'. She feared that if Kevin were to be allowed to express other feelings, then she would also begin to feel things she didn't want to. We negotiated individual therapy for her (within adoption support services), recognizing that in order to bear Kevin's' trauma with him, she must first bear the extent of her own lived experience. She was able in the meantime to take something from the musical experience and interpret it for herself and her situation. Feeling grounded in the music provided emotional regulation for her as much as for Kevin. The embodied musical experience, created and shared between the three of us, gave Kevin a reparative maternal experience. He could now sense this, and additionally know that his adopter was safely being held.

Verbal psychotherapists (Siegel 2006) have referred to the 'window of tolerance' model, which describes three 'bands' of emotional experiencing. The top band is a state of hyperarousal, where too much emotion or sensation is expressed and experienced in the body. The bottom band is hypoarousal, which is experienced as a state of numbness, depression and disassociation. In the middle lies the 'window of affect tolerance' where while we feel, we can still think. It is a place of emotional regulation. It would have been easy to join Kevin and his mum in what I was experiencing as very hyperaroused states, but which might equally have been viewed as excited engagement. The significance of being needs-led and relating to the client's lived experience was that with *this* child at *this* moment, the music and behaviour were part of his hyperaroused state. To join in musically would have offered no containment for the overwhelming sensations he and his mum felt and were expressing. Instead, the provision of an emotionally regulating state, which he responded to and became attuned to, led to us all finding a more tolerant place, and experiencing relationship.

Within music therapy, then, both Kevin and his mum were perhaps able to experience something lost to them both in their early lived experiences. Loewald (1980, cited in Sletvold 2014, p.104; emphasis added) states:

> The Mother's flow of words does not convey meaning to or symbolize things for the infant...*but the sounds, tone of voice, and rhythm of speech are suffused within the apprehended global event...* while the mother utters words, *the infant does not perceive words but is bathed in sound, rhythm etc.*, as accentuating ingredients of a uniform experience.

Early attachment had been lost for both Kevin and his mum in traumatic experience, but in new musical experiencing they could be similarly 'bathed' in sounds and rhythm.

Self-narratives, enacted with metaphor and stories

Adopted children reveal themselves and their past narratives usually in musical metaphors, or symbolic play. To enable symbolism, I incorporate a small range of toys in my work. To engage with other equipment, such as toys, it is advisable that music therapists access additional training. In addition to instruments, I tend to use a small range of puppets which a child can use to explore something symbolically in a safely externalized way. There is also a baby doll available, which might be used symbolically for a child's sense of their own inner baby self. There are fleece blankets for children to curl themselves up in, or ask to be wrapped up in by their adopter (when they feel able to request maternal nurture and holding). The music therapy space offers experiences of playing and singing music, occasionally enhanced with puppets, the doll, and blankets, wherein early narratives might be shared.

CASE VIGNETTE: **ANTON**

Anton was barely four when he came to therapy, yet was described as extremely aggressive. Little was known of his very early life, other than a history of physical abuse, resulting eventually in his enforced removal and adoption placement. His adoptive parents were in their twenties and admitted that they hadn't really believed a young child like Anton could have any sense of his early lived experience. They needed considerable support from the wider adoption team to think about his aggressive attacks (especially on his adopted mother) as communications about his inner state, so that sense-making about his music therapy could be appreciated.

Anton was one of many adopted children who seemed as if they wanted to destroy both the room and me. Most of our early work was about finding a way to direct his physical violence away from bodily expressions and onto/into the instruments and music. He quite quickly began to know that he could do this and relished the containment finally provided for his rage. He came running into sessions, flailing all his limbs at the gong, before 'attacking' the piano by playing it with all his physical strength. There were two pianos in the room. Anton would try to hit anyone who tried to play sitting alongside him, or who rhythmically joined him. Instead, on my piano I began to match his thumping and hitting movements, but with more containment, and held in strong musical structures of both rhythm and chords. Anton's rhythms were jagged, resisting any attempt to be joined musically. Each week, I would at first meet the fragmented nature of his play, but at some point, bring myself into a steady regular pulse. Over time, Anton became able to join me in music, still playing the piano extremely loudly, but with the aggression now having structured form. Gradually we became able to play strong, steady chords together. It felt like emerging from a fight, and now he could settle.

Anton then used his piano to hide behind. He took a baby dragon puppet, placed it on his right arm, and lay down, listening to me playing. He then made the dragon 'play' the piano and resumed with his right hand the inchoate music we began with, but began swapping and using his left hand to play in new softer quieter ways. Two parts of Anton were revealed: a quieter little boy who craved connection, but also an 'angry dragon' part who insisted on disrupting and spoiling things.

As this play evolved over time, I wondered if Anton, like many adopted children, unconsciously sensed rejection from his birth mother. Even children with histories of abuse that necessitated removal can come to believe that they must have done 'something wrong' for their parent to 'allow' them to be taken away. Was Anton fearful that he was really bad, monstrous, even dragon-like, and that his feelings of rage and anger had made one set of parents give him up? If so, was he terrified of the same happening with his adopters, and yet was his violence and destruction likely to bring about that which he most feared? Did he think his 'badness' could also destroy me, in music therapy?

I incorporated and shared some of my growing sense-making of Anton by beginning to sing a 'dragon song'. The song had a steady holding beat, and a regular repeating chordal pattern. The sung narrative was about a dragon who was very, very scared and who longed to play with others, but when he tried to do this he couldn't control all the sad and angry feelings inside, so he hid instead. Anton lay on the floor, behind his piano, listening to me, then asked for the song to be repeated, and made the dragon puppet enact it. Talking later with the adoption team, we thought involving Anton's adoptive dad (who had not become so afraid of Anton) in music therapy might help. Dad beautifully engaged in our next session using an 'adult dragon' puppet. He stated that the dragon was looking for a baby dragon, but knew that the baby dragon was very scared, so would not force him out of hiding and safety but would gently wait. Gradually, Anton began to let his right arm emerge from behind the piano, followed by the rest of Anton's body! Baby dragon stopped playing aggressive music, and instead joined Anton, Dad and me in steady pulsed song-making (and sense-making). In time, his adopted father was able to hold and cuddle baby dragon (still on Anton's arm of course!) who relished such contact.

Children with lived experiences like Anton's find incredibly creative ways to reveal their internal belief that they are 'bad' from birth and beyond redemption. It is not sufficient to verbally tell a child their belief is false; their feeling state needs to be recognized, held, and played with, before offering opportunities for transformation and toleration of possible new narratives. Anton later worked around anger and sadness when he acknowledged that he was not bad, and instead it was terrible that bad things had been done to him. We are likely to encounter musical dragons and monsters when we work in adoption, and being able to welcome and hold them in containing musical forms makes feeling states shareable, less dangerous and, therefore, less necessary to be acted out.

Maternal transference narratives

Maternal transference has been a theme for many adopted children, unsurprisingly. This may have been expressed in ways such as those illustrated above (Anton), or may have been more directly aimed at the music therapist.

CASE VIGNETTE: **LEON**

Eight-year-old Leon was born with a physical disability which meant he was not mobile and needed to attend sessions in his wheelchair. He had also suffered life-threatening injuries from his birth parents. His physical body held much traumatic memory. Initially in music therapy, he would constantly conflate past and present, including enactments of aspects of his early life narrative, and the whole experience showed how uncontained he felt. His trauma was alive and so I needed to work to ensure he had both space to express how he had experienced the world (especially as a defenceless baby, and with much of his experience residing in the body-mind), and regulation to return to the here and now. The behaviour and mood of children can change instantaneously, often in flashbacks where trauma is relived and experienced as isolated and sensorial. Leon would state indefatigably that his male classroom teacher and I were his birth parents, and any minor changes in our embodiment would resonate strongly with him, igniting memories of trauma.

CASE VIGNETTE: **MICHAEL**

Michael, similarly to Leon, would sometimes look at me and say, 'you've changed' and insist that something I had done, in a brief moment, had made me 'different'. He would say I was like his birth mum (from whom he had been removed due to her drug misuse). In micro-moments of transferential feeling, something in my state was highly evocative for Michael. This transference felt useful at times, but at others became too distressing for Michael, when an experience had the quality of a flashback in its evocation of emotional states associated with early terrifying memories. Scared Michael would tell me I was 'a bad mummy'. Children sometimes use such reactions to experiment with enacting fantasies about their birth family and early life, but require containment and affect regulation to ground them afterwards. Michael's pain (arising from pre-verbal experience) was wordless, so I suggested that together we played out more safely what the feelings were. He directed very angry and dissonant music towards me, deliberately wanting to make me feel bad. Desperately wanting to get rid of the feelings evoked, he projected them onto me, as representing his birth mother. I met his music with long, loud, steady drum beats, holding my own identity and simultaneously keeping both he and I rooted in the room, in the present.

CASE VIGNETTE: **LOUISE**

Louise was largely non-verbal due to her learning disability, but at times as we enjoyed relational music-making together. She would look at me, smiling, and call out 'mummy!'. In the music, there was a feeling that was good and could be welcomed, and which I sensed replicated the feelings of care her adoptive mum offered her.

With all children who experience an 'in the moment' transference, this is evoked by both the music and the embodied state between us. We need to be constantly vigilant and alert to this as 'change processes are affected to a great extent by the non-verbal body-emotional interaction between patient and therapist, whether conscious attention is paid to this interaction *or not*' (Sletvold 2014, p.xvii).

When we can't find or share the beat – adopted children's experiences with rhythm

As we have seen, children who come to music therapy may well have lost any sense of rhythmic relating, and seek to sabotage any potential for sharing rhythmic states. Some children present this differently; instead of seeking not to engage in shared rhythm, they contrive too hard to match and merge with the music therapist. We met Alice in Chapters 2 and 5 who learned compliance as a way of striving to keep her adoption from breaking down. The next two cases of Zara and Holly show similar engagement styles.

CASE VIGNETTE: **ZARA**

Zara had experienced one adoption breakdown. In music therapy, she sat silently on the floor, matching my body posture exactly. She would not initiate interaction but insisted on my choosing an instrument and beginning to play first. Whatever I chose, she would try to find an exact copy of for herself. Whatever rhythm I began, she would match exactly. If I experimented with rubato effects, she would copy me exactly. Zara was basically terrified of getting anything 'wrong' and upsetting me. Even some months into our work this was evident in her gong playing. She tentatively rested a beater on the gong, producing virtually no sound. She constantly monitored herself, playing so as not to cause too many vibrations.

CASE VIGNETTE: **HOLLY**

Holly also played extremely quietly and delicately, mirroring exactly what I played. She was placed with her younger sister, and her adoptive parents said there were no problems with the girls, other than what they described as their emotional 'neutrality'. It seemed that they (each having been in separate foster placements previously) were also monitoring themselves and each other. Staying eerily calm prevented any emotional expression emerging that felt out of their control, and which might cause them to do something bad and be rejected.

Both Zara and Holly gave me countertransference experiences of what it might be like to be their adoptive parent. I felt deeply sad for such little girls who denied themselves any spontaneity, and could not risk real relating. However, it was extremely frustrating to be constantly 'followed' musically. I identified this as transference when one of Zara's parents expressed frustration that Zara could not let her out of her sight. Zara felt that if she could not see her parents, they were lost to her. With both Zara and Holly (and their adopters present in the room), we experimented together with opening up a range of dynamics and rhythms, so these girls might experience themselves as 'other' in relating and know their entire authentic selves were wanted and welcomed in their new families.

Lullabies

I mentioned lullabies earlier, in Charmaine's narrative, but, more generally, lullabies are consistently brought into music therapy by adopted children. However, hearing a lullaby can feel very painful at first. The experience being offered in a sung lullaby is one that is nurturing and sustaining, and many children (needing to be self-contained and self-managing) will resist feeling vulnerable and needy, even as they might have had to as a baby. Some children have created their own lullaby words for our sessions, and asked me to sing with them as they wrapped themselves up in a blanket. The lilting rhythm and repetition of lullaby can evoke a feeling of safety, and also relaxation (which is why lullabies work!). Often, lullaby lyrics have a very dark undertone. Many adopted children reveal a felt sense of being 'dropped' in early life (either by describing this, or by symbolic revelation in music or play). 'Rock-A-Bye Baby' (which is perhaps the most adoption-related lullaby I can imagine!) contains the lyric 'When the bough breaks the cradle will fall, down will come baby, cradle and all' and has been brought into many sessions. The narrative is catastrophic, but is made bearable in a musical structure or container.

Finding the unsung lyrics – words contained in music

Lyrics have been very important in the pre-composed music that some children have brought into their sessions, as we saw with Joe's music therapy in Chapter 1. For Joe, both the lyrics and musical elements were of equal importance for him as he shared his unconscious lived experience.

CASE VIGNETTE: JOE

Joe brought contemporary pop songs to sessions and self-accompanied his singing on piano. I wondered if the pre-composed music was a defence against playing more risky improvised music, but my supervisor suggested that as everything happening in the room was important, so were these lyrics. Joe repeatedly sang (with huge focus, gaze and intensity) a lyric about a wild wind smashing glass. Joe had been removed from his birth mother, aged two, following an incident when his birth father had attempted to kidnap him from her. His birth father had entered the house, smashing Joe's ground floor bedroom window with a brick. We believed (I, his adopted mum, and the adoption team) that Joe had an unconscious embodied memory of this pre-verbal event. The lived experience of trauma was embodied, and able therefore somehow now to be brought into music therapy. Joe was desperate (during his transition through adolescence) to learn more of his birth family origins and began to trace his birth mum. The songs he used changed and included lyrics about not being a 'real' son to his adopters, and also the desire that his birth mum knew that his pain did not end when she gave him away. All of the lyrics he wanted to use were available in contemporary pop ballads.

CASE VIGNETTE: **LEON**

Leon often sang his self-composed song, which he titled: 'I just don't want to be adopted'. He feared talking about this with his adoptive parents because he experienced ambivalence about loving them, which he perceived as simultaneously rejecting his birth mother. In music therapy, he sang about how he loved and hated me, always later seeking reparation for expressions of his hatred. Breaks in music therapy were experienced very badly. He devised a repertoire of 'punishing songs' which he sang to me on return, first punishing me for abandoning him, but then seeking to mend the rupture. Such lyrics originated in his feelings about his birth mother, and his hatred for her abandonment, coupled with fears that his badness was the cause of her abandonment. Desperate to control our relationship, he showed me how rejecting and controlling he needed to be. Leon's early lived experience as a disabled baby who additionally suffered physical abuse meant he felt powerless. In music therapy, his pre-verbal unconscious material could be held. Gradually, he could risk attuned states happening between us in improvisational music-making, where both body and mind could 'speak' and be heard. Music therapy, therefore, is an extremely valuable modality where metaphors of an adopted child's internal world might be revealed through both sensory symbolic play and evolving song narratives.

The music of silence

Finally, silence has played an enormous part in music therapy with adoptees. Music comes out of silence. Music starts with silence. Silence is the counterpart to any sound. Silence can have a whole range of qualities at differing times. I am silenced by adopted children, who cannot allow themselves to have anything good offered to them in therapy, so 'shut me up'. Instruments are removed, or my hands are literally pushed off the piano. One child covered my mouth when I tried to sing (my voice being the one instrument that couldn't be removed or thrown or broken). Children who have been silenced by trauma need a music therapist who can understand something of this silencing experience, yet it is frustrating when, week on week, we are prevented from playing. Not only are we frustrated musically, we may also carry projections from the child who denies succour and nurture. These are situations where we need robust supervision.

Occasionally after music-making, some children have sought to share silence with me. There is as much attunement occurring in some of these moments as there is in the music. One little boy, near the end of three years of music therapy, lay wrapped in a blanket looking at me. After a protracted and comfortable silence, he said (looking at my treble clef nose piercing!): 'A music flew into your nose and it helps you help me'. Such moments, arising out of silence, enable some of the goodness of relating to be internalized so it can be taken into life beyond therapy. This is what we hope can be the eventual experience for all adoptees, which they take into their own placements, and might go some way to explaining why placements have endured.

Chapter 9

Resonances of the Music Therapist's Self in Intersubjective Relating

THE SIGNIFICANCE OF THERAPISTS' LIVED EXPERIENCES OF ADOPTION

The music therapist's own subjectivity within resonant intersubjective relating with clients is seldom examined, yet plays a 'significant role in the co-construction of any therapeutic trajectory' (Kuchuck 2014, p.10). If resonating relationships are vital for providing a felt experience of intersubjective fit in music therapy, we must, as Driver (2013, p.29) encourages, 'examine ontological theories of both clients *and therapist's* states within the therapeutic encounter'. This chapter focuses on the significance of the music-therapist-self in psychoanalytic, attachment and trauma informed, embodied relational music therapy with adoptees. It explores how music therapists might first be enabled to offer therapeutic witnessing of early trauma using musical presence that can then enable adoptees to reveal their inner worlds in a way that increases understanding of presenting attachment difficulties. In order to do this, music therapists need to be aware of their own attachment and trauma experiences, as their clients will draw heavily on their own material, especially if this material resonates. Music therapists who are adoptees or adopters themselves ask about 'how' the work I have been evolving can be attempted, because they want to contribute to a field in which they have lived experience. This chapter (and indeed book) cannot purport to offer a simple 'skillset' for intersubjective relating, but rather focuses on the unavoidable significance of the therapist-self. It explores what self-developments may be required to embark on this work, especially when we share lived experiences of adoption with our clients.

The basic premise for this chapter is an acceptance that a music therapist's own past traumas will inevitably affect the musical relationship with a client and will 'disturb' it in some way. We are hopeful that any such disturbance is helpful to the client. Alaane (2016), however, states the risks of working in adoption, because working with any trauma leaves us 'in danger of becoming traumatized and depressed…especially when confronted by great losses. Traumas and losses make music therapists more vulnerable, so we have to work to integrate our own traumas and vulnerabilities within our self-experience and personality' (p.37). Similarly, Austin (2009) considers trauma from the wounded therapist's perspective, concluding that the therapist is an 'instrument' that, in acknowledging and owning their own lived experience, might make sense of other material which constitutes the client's transference and projections.

An intersubjective music therapy

I have described in the preface and elsewhere my 'lived experience' of the 'adoption community' and that professionals working within this community are desired and sometimes even required to have 'lived experience' of adoption. However, earlier chapters challenged the assumption that any or all lived experience might be made use of in the therapeutic service of our clients. As music therapists, one reason we undergo therapy ourselves in training is to enable us to become more self-aware, and more able to bring to consciousness potentially unhelpful resonances with our clients. If we seek to work with clients with similar lived experiences, these might arouse 'personal identification during intersubjectivity which carries potential for un-self-aware enactments' (Driver 2013, p.32). Therapeutic resonances with our clients must therefore be explored to safeguard (in as much as this is possible) against this, and our experiences worked with enough to enable us to become more, perhaps 'wounded healers' (a description attributed to Jung). Jung believed that an analyst is compelled to treat others because the analyst himself is wounded. The 'analysed wounds' of the client affect 'the wounds of the analyst'. The analyst either consciously or unconsciously passes this awareness back to the client, causing an unconscious relationship to take place.

Because our medium of music in itself provides empathic, unconscious, emotional resonances existing at neurobiological, social and cultural levels (De Waal 2012), music has a vast potential for enabling fertile, creative change, but can also potentially engender complex relating where we are caught up unconsciously in enmeshment and enactment. Marks-Tarlow (2008) discusses how to avoid 'pitfalls of enactment', and suggests we can capitalize instead on the strengths of resonant dynamics by the music therapist engaging in her own process of psychotherapy/analysis and receiving robust supervision.

What seems obvious, but yet has been missed perhaps somewhat in music therapy literature, is that music therapists are embodied human beings creating sounds from the body as they engage in playing music and co-creating improvisations with clients. Music is made with the body and emanates from the body (as in singing). Trevarthen (2009) describes how the inherent musicality that he perceives in the earliest days of human life comes about via embodied relating: 'We have an innate communicative musicality that responds to the touches sights and sounds of human bodies intending and feeling emotional about the rewards and risks inseparable from acting and inventing in human company' (p.13). This inherent communicative musicality is the very thing that enables us to reach out and connect with what those who practice within a Nordoff Robbins (Nordoff and Robbins 1971) tradition might describe as our clients' 'inner music child'.

Our experience of our own embodied self does not really begin before birth, but rather when we enter the world and can begin to know our body in relation to an other. Lakoff (1987) states:

> Thought is embodied, that is, the structures used to put together our conceptual systems grow out of bodily experience and make sense in terms of it; moreover, the core of our conceptual systems is directly grounded in perception, body movements, and experiences of a physical and social character. (p.187)

We already know that adopted children who have experienced trauma experience an enormous disruption to the regularity of their 'communicative musicality', and any internal rhythmic sense helping to form conceptual systems is fractured and becomes disjointed as knowledge of the mother's relational body is lost. This is a further rationale for why a music therapy relationship, wherein sound-making cannot be separated from embodied relating, is well placed for working with adoptees.

Rhythms of relating: enabling embodied musical intersubjectivity

Reich (1949/1972) stressed the relevance of the creative arts in understanding the pre-linguistic nature of emotional experience and expression. The pre-verbal separation trauma known by all adoptees is such a pre-linguistic experience:

> The beginnings of living functioning lie much deeper and beyond language... Music is wordless and wants to remain that way. Yet music gives expression to the inner movement of the living organism and listening to it evokes the sensation of some inner stirring... The wordlessness of music is described as...the deepest expression of feeling (that is) incapable of being put into words... Deep feeling is identical with having contact with the living organism beyond the limitations of language. (p.359)

I would add that as well as listening to music, the involvement of two human embodied people actually playing music together is wordless, 'self-embodied-in-relationship', and can be therefore potentially revealing of unconscious material.

CASE VIGNETTE: JOE

Joe was previously described in Chapters 1 and 8. His preference for pop songs that contained ostinato and circling repeating chordal patterns seemed to offer for him reparation of lost early experiences of being held and rocked. Although while playing contemporary pop he would engage in postures of a young male pop star, I had an overwhelming sense of him as a vulnerable baby. As we worked with his songs (as described in Chapter 8), Joe engaged in sense-making that he might somehow be singing about himself. Eventually, we were able to have conversations about what was known of his early lived experience. Joe already knew this in his body and had brought it to therapy unprocessed, where a combination of the musical elements utilized and attuned sensitivity to his material led to a profound move from unconscious to conscious awareness.

Chapter 6 describes how, in order for such work to occur, music therapists need to engage in 'deep listening'. Sletvold (2014, p.137; emphasis added) describes how this is an embodied task: 'When the sharing and communication of emotions takes place *largely through our own and our patients body movements*, and this process is mostly relational it raises the issue…of *a different type of listening*.' So, music therapists need to listen to much more than the music. It is insufficient to focus on the melody, tone, timbre, rhythm and so on alone. Indeed, as Nebbiosi and Federici-Nebbiosi (2008, p.223; emphasis added) write:

> We must be able to *listen with all senses* to our patient's movements, recognizing the rhythmic forms of posture, facial expressions, alternations of words and silence. In short, understanding another person, and ourselves in relation to another person, is achieved not just through verbal and/or visual language, but also through *the language of movements* that gives form and allows to share *the effects of a relationship*.

In their later work, Federici-Nebbiosi and Nebbiosi (2012, p.214; emphasis added) show how 'rhythmic experience is basically relational and plays a fundamental role in creating dialogue *between ourselves and our bodies as well as between us and other people'*. They describe ways in which the co-creation of *rhythm* is an important element for the co-creation of *meaning*, as well as a factor promoting an ability to better get to know and understand the complex implicit languages of body movements and facial expressions to which contemporary psychoanalysis is assigning an increasing value. For music therapists, rhythm is of course one of the most fundamental musical elements we might use and extremely valuable because 'subjective emotions all have special rhythms…a particular breath, heartbeat, muscle tension… Rhythmic forms have an exquisitely interactive value and…a specific relational function' (ibid.).

However, as we have seen in earlier chapters, adoptees may struggle to surrender to the musical rhythms of the other, and thereby share a sense of pulse. The experience can be terrifying for adoptees who have experienced the loss of that fundamental rhythm of self-narrative in early life. Sharing rhythm involves letting go of something of the self to become able to merge in the space between music therapist and client that is filled with music. Federici-Nebbiosi and Nebbiosi (2012) agree that 'rhythmic experience always entails surrendering to something other than us and which may become part of us only when we surrender to it' (p.216). Almost all of the adoptees I have worked with have at the commencement of the work avoided getting rhythmically close. One little girl began playing an apparently strong rhythm, which I felt could be easily joined with, yet she 'slipped through my fingers' whenever I tried to play with her. I realized that although she possessed a sense of rhythm, it was less coherent than it appeared and there was no sense of internal pulse. She could not, in Winnicott's terms, allow herself to freely play. Sletvold (2014) describes learning to share rhythm as being like learning to dance together, 'Therapeutic interaction would depend on the form of the dance and on how the analyst is able to lead the dance with a particular patient.' (p.136) I would add that in client-led music therapy *we need to be equal partners in the musical dance emerging between us; sometimes leading and sometimes following*. We also must remain aware that some children might need to say, 'I can't dance, don't ask me'.

Determining who leads the relational dance, and in what way, leads us on to thinking about possible manifestations of transference and countertransference. Geltner (2012), writing about countertransference, describes language and feelings as two channels of human communication, cognitive and emotional. For music therapists, music-making offers an additional 'channel'. It shares some similarity perhaps with language, but is different in that it intrinsically contains within it more emotional states. Geltner draws on Winnicott's (1949, p.23) description of 'objective countertransference' but develops it into what he defines as 'subjective countertransference': 'Subjective transference is a feeling that is induced in the analyst by the patient's emotional communications and is a repetition of a feeling that originated in the patient's emotional life history.' Sletvold (2014) further develops this, describing an 'induced and personal countertransference' for feelings originating in the analyst's own life history.

These developments in thinking about countertransference are helpful in considering the significance of the therapist in a musical intersubjective relationship. The therapist first has a self, which has come into being via its embodied relationships. Sletvold (2014, p.30; emphasis added) describes it thus: 'Sensations and feelings derived primarily from our own bodily reactions constitute in my terminology the *embodied self-experience, or embodied subjectivity*.' He then goes on to how intersubjectivity might be experienced in embodied relating:

> Intersubjectivity is the ability to experience (feel, sense) some of the mind processes of others, shaped by our unique capacity as humans to simulate and imitate the experience of the other... Embodied identification is therefore critical for understanding intersubjectivity as something no longer based on a cognitive conception of theory of mind, but *rather embodied intersubjectivity*. (Sletvold 2014, p.81; emphasis added)

As a music therapist, then, my body is in the room, and engaged in embodied acts of playing and listening, therefore I am relating from the embodied self, *whether I am aware and acknowledge this or not*. I recognize this is essential because 'change processes are affected... by the non-verbal body-emotional interaction between patient and therapist, whether conscious attention is paid to this interaction or not' (Van der Kolk 2014, p.14).

The following two examples highlight musically embodied communications of clients, and how they were managed at the time. They illustrate why the music therapist must be alert to their own processes and exposure of any personally painful material.

CASE VIGNETTE: **KATY**

Katy was playing the piano and singing a song she made up about physical abuse she had experienced which had resulted in scarring on her arm. I sat alongside her, supporting her melodic expressions with sustaining chords. Katy sang about being hit by her birth mother, resulting in her scars, then sang that not only could I see her scars, but 'you know because you have scars too'. Katy had no knowledge of my narrative, yet somehow had unconsciously tapped into it. I continued to hold the music while thinking of a response, and gradually introduced a counter melody line with the words 'you have scars too', as a way of recognizing some similarity between us, but also stressing our difference so the risk of any unhelpful merging was reduced.

CASE VIGNETTE: **GEORGE**

At the age of 16, George had secretly traced his birth sister and subsequently his birth mother via social media. His sister had been delighted to be 'found' by him and helped him to search for their birth mother who, once found, rejected both of them totally. George had not told me this had been happening but came to a session and drummed continuously, furiously and loudly, refusing to let himself be 'found' at all in the music. The music felt extremely painful and rejecting to receive and hold. In supervision, aspects of my own painful lived experience of rejection were identified honestly, and then this was further explored in my own therapy. Then I was able to share with George the sadness I felt at being shut out of his music which had previously been relational. George shouted, 'Well, I'm shutting you out because she shut me out!' He then revealed his secret finding of and rejection by his birth mother. We were then able to involve his adopted mother in some shared music-making and his adopted mother was able to help him manage painful feelings. Later his adoptive mum encouraged him to try again to meet his birth mum, but this time with support and stability.

Problems of shared lived experience, and possible solutions

There are two potentially problematic issues for music therapists who identify closely with clients' lived experiences, as identified by Alaane (2016):

- The dynamics arising directly in the work in the moment.
- The therapist's own traumatic experience which may or may not be contained.

Alaane acknowledges that dynamics such as 'transference, counter transference and other unconscious stimuli' encountered by clients can equally arise in the music therapist, who is not immune. He suggests first that to manage such dynamics we need supervision. The regulating body for music therapists in the UK, the Health and Care Professionals Council (HCPC), stipulates that all music therapists should have clinical supervision, yet does little to qualify what type of supervision, or what frequency, is useful. Supervision can provide a space to think about what we contribute to the 'space between' self and client. In a robust trusting supervisory relationship, we have a permissive, accepting space to learn about ourselves and our relating in the therapy room. Second, Alaane says that personal psychotherapy might enable deeper explorations, bringing to consciousness parts of our motivations for our work. If these might be safely owned and known, they become less likely to 'trip us up', and offer some solution to the problems of working with lived experience.

Acknowledgment and conscious recognition of our own

attachment and trauma experiences reduce the risk that music therapy will be complicated in ways that are unhelpful to our clients by our own lived experience. 'Counter-emotions from patients must be scrutinized...and considered in interpretations of clinical observations' (Alaane 2016, p.34). The purpose of this is to be able to own and acknowledge our trauma so that it does not 'contaminate' client material, but I would stress it is also equally importantly that our work does not cause us further difficulties for ourselves. We are working with powerful 'in the room experiences' of transference and countertransference in potent relationships which risk evoking shared material, and care of both the client and our own self matters. It is a necessary act of self-care to set aside specific places to think deeply about this, making sure we are protected and safe in the work. Paying attention to our feeling states enables containment, which can minimize any complications similar traumatic experience might bring to the work. In my own practice, both my supervisor and therapist have enabled me to think in order to become, as much as is possible, a therapeutic 'instrument' of integrity and authenticity.

The art therapist Helen Greenwood has described a concept of a reticulum of containers (Greenwood 2011), which has become a way for me of defining how we might manage lived experience. A music therapist is contained primarily by their own creativity, then by their supervisor, and then by their therapist. Greenwood's image of a bowl being placed within another bowl, then within another bowl is a helpful visual metaphor for a manner of holding that sustains our deeper work. If therapists are wounded healers, we are 'bowls' with cracks and fissures that we hope have been mended but remain visible. We work from this place, not as perfect all-knowing therapists, but retaining awareness of our humanity and vulnerability. Acceptance of this opens and softens us up, making us more able to engage with the 'other' as fully human, leading to a recognition of the connectedness we have to each other, and compassion for the difficulties of our fellow humans. This is imperative if we are members of the adoption community we choose to work in.

It is my sense that the 'reticulum of containing' we can experience both as a client in therapy and as a supervisee can provide us with experience that corresponds to a 'nurturing mother' function. Positive relationships over time with our therapist/supervisor offer continuity in relationship. Clients need holding from us of a quality which might provide their first ever experience of what Winnicott describes as 'gaze' (discussed in Chapter 3).

What is absolutely clear from Winnicott is that we can only truly encounter others when our own selves are not getting in the way, or when our lived experiences are not projected onto the client. Winnicott's 'gaze' might be experienced at times in a session between music therapist and client as a literal eye-to-eye gaze, and I have described also the possibility of a musical gaze, but I feel this also translates into music therapy as what I call 'the fundamental tone of being in relationship' (Gravestock 2019b). By this I mean the way we can musically hold 'gaze' with clients when micro-moments of attuned music-making occur. This implies an emotional capacity in the music therapist, who must be able to hold the client's musical experience *without detracting from it or turning it into something else*. If the music therapist has difficulty being there with the client's reality, a meta-message will be communicated which discourages further exploration. It can be very easy and even seductive in the countertransference to detract from the client's experience or turn it into something else when our own material is not being held safely somewhere. Yet our personal adoption and trauma material can subconsciously add something positive to the sense of intimate attunement between us. It can become present to clients, either in their projections and fantasies about us, or perhaps even resonating unconsciously somehow in the space between us, in the shared musical 'gaze'. Clients can then feel more connected with a sense of having a self, by being with another *who validates that self,* which an intuited sense of shared lived experience can provide. Isolation is reduced and greater intimacy with both self and other is enhanced.

Historically, much psychoanalysis has constructed the therapist as being 'all knowing' and the client as 'not knowing' about what is actually their own life. The client's 'unconscious material' is foregrounded and thought about in the therapeutic relationship. Power and knowledge reside with the client, who is seen ideally as 'opaque' in relating. Yet what we have learned about the embodiment of playing music shows that the music therapist manifests in an unconscious world too, even if attempting to remain opaque. The embodied self cannot be hidden, and is especially evidenced in music-making. This significance of the body in music therapy led me to explore more about what happens in those musical spaces co-created between therapist and client which are enactments of embodied intersubjectivity. Standard descriptions of music therapy techniques such as 'matching' and 'mirroring' no longer seemed adequate. Something more was being asked for consideration – something that required working with an embodied presence beyond a conscious cognitive matching.

Music therapy as embodied play and presence

Alaane (2016) seemingly provides a definition of embodied play in music therapy:

> Music is not an object; rather that I feel, hear and sing music *with my flesh. My body is the object that is felt, heard and sung.* The music reveals life in itself...we perceive and know the world subjectively through our bodies. (p.15)

Similarly, the words of T.S Eliot (1943), 'You are the music, while the music lasts' (p.20) contain something about music existing only in a temporal ephemeral form *while we are making it with our active bodies*. In art therapy, clients create images which are tangible not just in the therapy room, but when taken by the therapist to supervision. Music does not exist outside the original experience of playing it in the same way, even when it is recorded. Although we listen back to an experience, the act of listening is itself a new experiencing of the music, separated by time from the original experience. Embodied musical relationships can exist in time and space only. Music therapy, then, provides a *total embodied temporal experience* where material can be revealed, addressed and survived. The aware music therapist with lived experience of adoption, by allowing access to her own trauma, is neither swallowed nor destroyed by the client's reality, but remains humanly and affectively present, while retaining access to a meta perspective. Feelings in the music therapist's body might then be identified as her own, or as projected material from the client. Chapter 6 described how shared music-making requires a 'presence' which is ever alive to awareness of the *quality* of relationship *in the present time*. Music similarly exists in present time and co-creating therapeutic *presence* demands that *both* client and therapist become part of each other's worlds, so *both* are touched and changed. As Stern (2004; emphasis added) describes it:

> The present moment I am after is *the moment of subjective experience as it is occurring*, not as it is later re-shaped by words. What is shared in a moment of meeting is an emotional lived story. *It is physically, emotionally, and implicitly shared* not just explicated. (p.xiii)

The qualitative musical feel of implicitly shared intersubjective experience is experienced in rhythmical attention that involves the subjective felt senses of both client and therapist, encountered in what we so simply call 'playing together'. We experience true intersubjectivity in music therapy with adoptees when our own embodied musical self is fully present in the room. Earlier chapters describe case examples of adoptees seeking to silence the music therapist, or deny the music therapist self-agency, or deny anything that might be available for them in musical relating. By controlling playing, choosing instruments, telling us how to play, dictating rhythm and so on, adoptees can either idealize or violate music therapists. But, when we survive such projections and are eventually able to play separately, as a self-in-relationship, a sense of musical conversation emerges. Now we develop relational rhythmic relating.

In adoption work that is informed by attachment and trauma, we need at times to play with intensity, but we equally must be able to regulate our own playing, experimenting musically with closeness and distance within intersubjectivity. Wilkinson (2006) describes the 'look/look away' interaction involved in sharing visual gaze that people with attachment difficulties must feel in control of in psychotherapy. This is because the continued gaze of the therapist can be too much to bear at times, as within such gaze other early memories may be evoked. Similarly, in relational music-making we need to balance 'sound-making' or musical gazing ('look') with silence ('look away'). Then clients can lead the way in sense-making about qualities of warmth, similarity and empathy experienced within musical intersubjectivity. Clearly, we must be in the musical relational experience as much as our client. Yet equally we must remain aware of our own attachment and loss histories and traumas, without this impacting in a way which might lead clients to feel restrained or lacking in permission to reveal themselves. Interactive-being-with, while music-making, and also simultaneously reflecting, matching and mirroring our client's states requires momentary distance at times from intense interpersonal involvement. Maintaining the necessary balance has been described as having 'one foot in the river, with the other firmly on the river bank'.

It seems that when we become present and involved with clients, responding to and with them 'in the moment' of musical relating, we open up co-created space for what I call 'micro-moments of attunement' (Gravestock 2019a) to occur. These are enabled first within the music that is being made between us: musical elements both played and heard in relational experiences of co-creating rhythm, melody, timbre, pulse, silence, tempi, dynamic and so on. Second, they exist in the relationship, and what we might pick up and understand as transference, or countertransference. Music and relationship together reveal the internal world functioning of a client, and unconscious relational processes such as projections. Third, there is the neurobiology of what is occurring between two 'brain-body-minds' as expressed in embodied relating in the room. Neurobiology offers helpful insights into patterns of relating that emerge, such as when the client and therapist are matched and mirrored or not, when our breathing might regulate, or our bodies otherwise show evidence of intersubjectivity. Finally, the arising shared embodiment between client and therapist can be considered. The 'dance' of attachment, attunement, and entrainment might reveal unconscious aspects of early lived experience, resonating for both, and as we go on in time and relationship, might indicate changes and new relational enactments. Clearly, though, playing together reveals not just the inner world of a client *but also the music therapist's own internal world*, bringing into play unconscious processes between two 'brain-body-minds' in musical relationship.

As we attempt to tease apart these layers (which are of course inseparable, other than for such purposes of analysis) that occur within a single moment, we realize the rich complexity of the essence of musical relational attunement. As music therapists are caught in embodied musical interactions in the therapy, we are immersed in musical moments, and become an undeniable part of the sound world created. We play the music, we are in the music, and we might sing, move, dance and touch as we play. Some responding might be conscious and thought out to a certain degree, but for music therapy to 'work' and moments to really be described as attunement, we will not necessarily be aware and are simply 'doing it'! This is perhaps why it defies description! Yet this very 'doing' state is a product of all our lived experience, our knowledge and training, and many other elements that make us the music therapists we are.

Tributaries to an intersubjective 'lake'

An image arises in my mind of a lake when I think about the complexity of this musical intersubjective therapeutic relationship. The lake is the place where client and music therapist meet and play together. I envisage the lake fed by four tributaries to my work which might loosely be described as: the music, psychoanalytic thought, neurobiology, and embodiment theories. However, the lake itself is not clear in this image. It is deep, dark and muddied, sourced from other tributaries which are less explored, less known, including the client's unconscious, and the therapist's unconscious – indeed, all the experiences that make client and music therapist who they are to date, as they meet in this 'micro-moment'. It is in this far murkier territory that we meet and play.

Tributaries cause ripples in a lake as they meet, blend and become part of each other, creating something new and different together. Ripples or waves that meet establish what is known as a 'standing wave', a point of no movement, also called a node in wave theory. Perhaps this idea of 'nodes' is similar to 'micro-moments of attunement'? We experience similar points within our intersubjective music-making where clients meet us and for maybe even a single moment feel heard, held and understood. Out of this attuned experience can flow new reparative ways of relating.

Offering coherence and continuity of being is a fundamental aspect of a centred, responsive music therapist's self-system that we offer in our therapeutic musical presence to clients. A provision of musical presence is evident when, in gentle awareness of the space between us and our client, information can be passed subliminally between us. Such presence has been described in previous chapters as the containing and holding power of listening; simply sitting beside a client provides an attending, waiting, reflecting, space of shared observed attention, wherein the client can experience themselves and their thoughts and feelings in the moment. It is within musical presence experienced with another that an adopted client might begin to experience being held, heard and musically gazed on by a therapist who shows empathic understanding of where the client has come from and now is. Music therapists offer this presence when they are alive to their own (especially adoption, attachment and trauma-related) material and are able to contain it sufficiently to be available in a deeply authentic manner.

Chapter 10

Lily

LEARNING FROM LIVED EXPERIENCE

The penultimate chapter of this book is comprised of a single in-depth case study. The aim of focusing in such detail on one case is to highlight various elements of my music therapy approach within the adoption context, as detailed in earlier chapters. I illustrate, through an analysis with a now extremely 'close-up lens' as it were, how such elements arise directly from client-led presentations, and in this case from one child's lived experience. The music therapy, which happened over an extended period of time, especially highlights how both client and music therapist came to experience a musical intersubjective relationship, wherein experiments with attachment style were enabled by many 'micro-moments of attunement'. This case study emphasizes the necessary long-term nature of much adoption work and why this amount of time is essential for engaging in relational music therapy with complex adoption/attachment difficulties. The reader has an overview of a relationship developing over time and how my underlying theoretical base continued to evolve in sense-making about the work with the child and parent.

Significant relational and musical moments in therapy concurred with written reflections that I received by email, offered spontaneously by the child's adoptive mother, Jilly. The emails underlined significant changes in attachment relationships outside the therapy room in Lily's wider life, which coincided with moments of attunement felt and experienced within the music therapy.

Jilly has given permission for the story of her lived experience of adopting Lily, and Lily's subsequent music therapy with me, to be shared in this book. Together we hope that music therapists, and others working therapeutically within the adoption community, may also learn from Lily's lived experience.

Referral and funding process

First referred to music therapy aged three, Lily had an initial year of work (funded via her regional adoption agency, Coram), and subsequently a further two years were granted (funded via the Adoption Support Fund). As her needs were extremely complex, the local authority lead for support after adoption, together with me, argued for and obtained a further three years' funding from the Adoption Support Fund (see Chapter 4). Lily therefore was engaged in music therapy from the age of three until nine.

As mentioned in Chapter 1, sometimes when a child is born with disabilities, parents cannot (for whatever reasons) face the lifelong implications of care that will be required. Therefore, some disabled children are relinquished to adoption because of being born with disabilities. It was in such circumstances that Lily was placed into the care of the local authority on birth, and adopted later. She had a diagnosis of Down syndrome, with complex associated (potentially life-threatening) physical problems. Because her disability narrative was inseparable from her adoption narrative, her re-attachment needs in placement were huge, rooted as they were in her very identity as a disabled child.

Imagining Lily

Lily's story began with her birth, which we could not share with her or fully know about. I often write imaginary narratives about new clients as a creative reflection, from the perspective of the baby that the client would have been. A referred adoptee may be two years old, or a young person of 20, so I try to reach, in an act of imagination, to the baby that they once were, as a means of giving recognition to the baby self that still remains within.

Baby Lily's imagined narrative

Nine months I have grown here. I am rocked in the rhythms of my mother's breathing. She feels my movements and cradles her hands around her belly to sing to me. I am held. But then. Screaming. Rushing. Chaos. And in a floodtide, I am pushed out into blinding light and noise… And I am dropped. I fall down and down and down forever. No hands hold me, no voice soothes me, no eyes gaze into mine. My mother's voice screams 'NOOOOOO! Take it away! I cannot bear it'.

The earliest experience

This narrative that I ascribe in imagination to Lily's lived experience was written when I first read the bald facts contained in her referral. Lily was a planned second pregnancy and there were no concerns throughout regarding the health of the birth mother or Lily. It was therefore a surprise to all concerned when she was born with Down syndrome. Her birth family had minimal engagement with her and a decision was made by her birth parents that she would be relinquished for adoption. She was later placed with a single female adopter.

We have learned throughout this book how neuroscience and observational studies have shown that babies are aware of their environment and responsive to sensory experience, even in the womb. Bonding and attachment processes begin in utero, as a mother's voice can be learned and orientated to. Lily therefore experienced enormous trauma by being rejected as she was born, and responded to this rejecting relational experience by psychologically protecting and defending herself for many years. Chapter 1 described the challenges of using a relational music therapy approach when working within such painful adoption narratives. Sutton (2002) describes how music therapists' own histories can be exposed when engaged in this work, therefore my own supervision and therapy supported it. Lily required deep thinking that focused on the nature of the holding environment, the significance of the mother-infant relational field, and her earliest life dynamics.

In all adoption work discussed throughout this book, there is explicit recognition that short-term therapy might risk replicating the experiences and inner worlds of children when they form a relationship with a therapist only to have it severed too soon. Long-term work alone offers the time and space necessary for sufficient containment and holding. I follow the recommendations of Knox (2011) who advises the necessity of staying in the sharing of traumatic experience to establish different relationship forms that can only over time move towards integration.

We know that free improvisation in music therapy with adopted people, especially those with early life trauma, is valuable because working in micro-moments of musical relating can viscerally open up the whole attachment process. Improvised music (as this book discusses) can reveal an adoptee's internal world figures, making attachment shapes and patterns audible and visible. Music therapy powerfully affects intra- and inter-personal responses because it exists as a temporal and affect-laden form. Neuroscience, evidencing brain plasticity, shows the capacity for development of new neural pathways. This gives hope for relational change and provides a rationale for advocating for long-term therapy with adoption. However, the nature of being human cannot be solely reduced to genetic, neurological or developmental processes but must encompass the whole of human experience. Music therapy with Lily addressed such aspects.

Evolving relationship

At the point of referral, it was hoped that music therapy might help adults caring for Lily to access her internal world, while providing a means for her of communicating herself to the outside world. Her version of Down syndrome resulted in considerable neurodevelopmental delay. Aspects of her condition might also have been due to emotional reasons, but we agreed that these must not obscure her very real organic difficulties, and music therapy was a chosen modality because it could work with both the physical and emotional. Lily's distress revealed itself in her behaviours, and it was hoped that music therapy might provide a safe place for her to articulate distress, and for it to be thought about, thus lessening her need to act out emotional states.

From the outset of our relationship it was obvious that Lily was indeed going to be able to use therapy! Right from the beginning, she arrived for each session with sheer determination to get into the room and begin to express herself. There was an urgency about her communications and her desire to relate. Happy from the outset to attend sessions unaccompanied (with mum sitting in the next-door room), she curiously explored all that my room had to offer.

Despite her overt desire and enthusiasm to engage, it became apparent that Lily, like many adoptees, manifested her trauma in her playing. Although she played continuously, and seemingly rhythmically, any felt sense of a musical connection would be immediately severed. Lily had learned very early on to exist alone, and being joined felt quite terrifying. Early sessions were chaotic and any music that did emerge was fragmented.

Winnicott's (1971) empathic holding environment, provided by the mother in early life, allows a baby to settle and explore in an undefended way the state of simply being. Such being-to-being connection allows the maternal relational field to attune to the baby's being, inner states and basic needs. The baby senses that in the mother's being they are acknowledged, accepted and loved. In the reflection provided by the mother's being, the baby learns about its own being and nature. Lily had lost any such early maternal holding, and the experience led to her believing she could exist only by herself. I was made to feel musically non-existent, (as indeed her birth mother had become to her). To risk true relatedness meant experiencing inter-being, which was too frightening. Severance of the maternal holding relational field meant Lily's basic needs as a baby were dramatically overridden. However, in a reparative musical relationship it was possible to provide a holding maternal aspect for her, in addition to that of her adopter.

Lily's survival tactic of pseudo independence meant she needed to be allowed room to discover things herself. She became quickly frustrated when she couldn't immediately work out how to play an instrument, yet gradually learned to tolerate frustration and ask for help. At first it was important to wait with her, allowing her to experience frustration, so gradually she could feel her vulnerability and need, developing a capacity to relinquish independence. It was important to maintain a stance that did not 'interfere or abandon' (see Chapter 6).

The impact of the traumatic loss of a mother (often the first attachment figure) can create serious attachment issues. Infants absorb overwhelming sensations of abandonment, while not yet possessing resources for language to process and assimilate their experience. Verrier's (1993; see Chapters 1 and 2) description of this is an 'emotional wound' which endures. Babies defend against their own needs, which are experienced as unmet. Although Lily was spoken about as a 'fiercely independent' child, it was painful to witness in reality a profoundly disabled tiny pre-school girl who had to exert such independence for survival. It was as if she had devised an impermeable skin around her.

From the first session, Lily began an enactment that continued for many weeks. She picked up any instrument and immediately rejected it by throwing it backwards over her shoulder, across the room. The gesture was so instantly dismissive and rejecting that I became immediately mindful of how she had been rejected at birth, and what a strong message her rejection now of my instruments was. The instruments (and by implication the relationship) had to be rejected before we even got started. I witnessed many weeks of what it felt like to be 'thrown away'. Knox (2011) has described such witnessing over time as necessary reflecting back of the affective state of a person as groundwork for the expression of trauma. Lily's adoption narrative was leading her to predict her current environment in the context of her trauma, and this was happening within her adoption placement also.

The first musical enactments of adopted children in music therapy are neither tidy nor beautiful. However, through their intrinsic sensory modality, they provide music that is an expression of an adoptee's narrative of being. 'Throwing away' that was met, witnessed and reflected back musically was experienced now by Lily within a holding environment. Hearing themselves reflected in musical relationship gives a vital sense to adoptees of being alive in the presence of another. Tuning in to all embodied aspects of our client's music-making, and holding it, can offer a new relational experience possibly like Bion's (1962/1984) maternal reverie. This experience of Lily allowing herself to exist in the heart and mind of another provided the beginnings for reparation of all that had been lost to her.

Lily's physicality as she played was lively and she used her body constantly. Sometimes this was obviously expressed in deliberate little dances she made up, but at other times there was more sense of her embodied states unconsciously 'sounding' her narrative. The body expresses unconscious earliest experiences, and adoptees might, in embodied musical relating, access memories of pre- and perinatal experiences held below consciousness at a cellular level but felt in musical playing as sympathetic vibrations, similar to those felt in very early experience (see Chapter 6). As music therapists, we can resonate musically with early memories, even if they lie below conscious awareness. Stern (2010) describes the embodied relational matrix out of which each individual human being both emerges and remains embedded. Lily's embodiment expressed, at levels beneath conscious awareness, her sensed dynamic intersubjective field.

Adopted children carry internalized knowledge of their early trauma, as Wilkinson (2010) describes (as seen in earlier chapters) as 'the old present'. In Lily's case, her body communicated her 'old present' and the trauma, rejection and losses she felt from her earliest moments. Her embodied expression needed to be met in the body of another, and could be understood in various theories that contribute to my approach. Playing music offered Lily, in Sutton's (2002, p.35) terms, an experience of herself 'embodied in sound and in silence'. Similarly, Pavlicevic's (1997) term dynamic form (describing ourselves portrayed in relation to another in sound) also descriptively encapsulates Lily's embodied play; or in Trevarthen's (2009, p.199) terms, Lily expressed her 'intrinsic motive pulse and audible gesture'. While she communicated in embodied states and dancing, I found music to mirror her actions, simultaneously meeting, witnessing and containing them. In neurobiological terms, therefore, I provided a 'mirror matching mechanism', or in Sletvold's (2014) terms embodied empathy. In music therapy, while we seek to relationally attune to our clients in improvisations, the embodied total experience can allow both body and mind to speak and to be heard. This provides a rationale for music therapy as a preferred modality for children such as Lily, where we work with very early trauma. Her internal world could be revealed through both evolving musical sounds, embodied dance and gesture, and later on in sensory symbolic play.

As Lily began to feel witnessed as she was, she was enabled to move from defended fragmented states to a more cohesive mode of being. Gradually, the music between us developed coherence with, for example, chord patterns and rhythmic structures becoming more regular and shaped. Lily's playing became more grounded and settled, less scattered and fragmentary. It was as if music offered her a stability she could now begin trusting, at least in part. Continued bodily engagement (for example, rocking with the music) allowed her to develop self-soothing. Very movingly on a couple of occasions she lay on the floor with a small instrument in her hands which she enjoyed exploring in a sensory way while allowing my music to support her. She would sing softly to herself in these times, seemingly caught up in a reverie-like state (Bion) that existed between us. She was learning to be 'alone in the presence of another' (Winnicott) which evidenced her growing attachments developing. This was supported by what her adopted mum was saying in emails.

Micro-moments of attunement were regularly experienced in musical relationship with Lily, and further evidenced how embodied intersubjectivity was being played out in the physicality and dynamics occurring in our playing music together. Her self-states could be matched and mirrored in musical dynamics, often also containing much laughter as we each experienced cross-modal attunement. When a song of Lily's creating moved from traumatic material into laughter and fun, I knew that the traumatic material had been held safely, witnessed and thought about in a new way. As Lily allowed another person to become present for her, she was able to settle into a more coherent affect function within the 'window of tolerance' (Chapter 8). Playing and singing together naturally invoked embodied states, aiding her emotional regulation.

Themes from Lily's music therapy common to adoption work

I shall now describe some ongoing and often repeated themes in Lily's music therapy that have also emerged fairly consistently in some form or another in other adoption work.

Supergirl

Sometimes Lily came to our sessions dressed as 'Supergirl'. This gave a strong message about her need still to feel competent and in control. Her play in character was more dominant and even contained intimations of aggression. Adoptees can take on the aspects of other such characters to play out differing states, but one step removed. There was a need for her to retain defences and not risk too much vulnerability, and this character provided a role to experiment with such defences. At times, she wanted to dance around me 'flying' while holding on to my hand. I simply sang the reflecting words 'round and round' as she experimented feeling both separate from and connected to me, physically and in song. She required a regular steady presence that she could literally hold on to in order to gather herself again for further development. Over some months, she veered between an apparent growing security in her relationships with others, and needing to revert to enactments of pseudo independence.

Hide and seek

Lily evolved games within sessions that I had to first learn and then follow (she was teaching me how to be needs-led!). She enjoyed using boomwhackers, bringing them to me one at a time and requesting that I hold them upright in front of my face. The more boomwhackers I held, the more my face was obscured from her view. From this evolved a game of peek-a-boo, a sort of hide and seek. This game has been so significant in the musical play of almost all adopted children I have worked with (and was similarly described as 'Fort! Da!' by Freud in 1920). I sang to her during this time about her 'finding' me as her music therapist, and likewise 'finding' her adoptive mother. She was delighted when I could be easily found in music, and laughed, showing me that she felt safe in her play and not frightened that I had temporarily vanished.

A similar 'Fort! Da!' game developed where Lily would place herself (standing) behind me while I knelt on the floor. As I sang, 'Where is Lily?', she enjoyed teasing me before coming into my view, thus allowing herself to be 'found'. I would sing 'You found me!' and she would giggle. Sometimes in play she would dance and twirl and launch herself into my lap, confident now that I would literally be physically present for her, and hold her. Again, I developed sung improvisations to include words about her 'finding' her adoptive mother, and her mother 'finding' her, aiming to encourage her to translate this experience to other contexts.

Look/Look away

Many adopted children struggle if they cannot visibly see their music therapist and struggle week to week to believe they will be held in mind. Some adoptees will need to retain a tangible reminder (such as a photograph of the music therapist) to enable them to manage. Yet, just as a child needs to know that they can see and be seen by a music therapist, there also needs to be space for them to not be seen, or to 'look away' (in Wilkinson's (2010) terms). Sufficient shared gazing is required for a child to feel contained, but not so much that she is overwhelmed. I learned to follow Lily's pacing and not over anticipate, as she constantly struggled to find autonomy and independence, while recognizing her need of others. Schore (1994) (see Chapter 6) demonstrated how gaze plays a crucial part in the development of a sense of self and of other, underpinning all relating developing from early relational lived experience. Transformational power, then, may be embedded in the most fleeting of affective interactions, and also in silence. The experience of silence juxtaposed with times of looking and 'sound gazing' has been an important part of many children's music therapy.

Attachment evolving with an adopter

Attachment that was happening within music therapy seemed to replicate Lily's evolving relationship with her adoptive mother. She was developing a sense that she had a very present adoptive parent who wanted to be with her, and who was available to her. I often felt a strong transference in music therapy when she expected me to be a rejecting mother, but was also relieved and pleased to find that I accepted her and enjoyed her play as it was. She became able to tolerate times of misattunement because of this, accepting that I would not always 'get it right' in my responses. The timing, spacing and reciprocity developing musically between us could encompass miscommunications, because there had been enough learned stability for me to make reparation when I did not totally understand her expressions. Again, her mother evidenced in her emails to me times at home when Lily was able to accept love and comfort from her.

Goodbye songs

In the second year of therapy we together evolved a 'Goodbye Song' which Lily relished. I do not routinely use either hello or goodbye songs, but this song was devised by Lily. She would place herself on the floor, lying on her tummy in front of me and looking up to be sung to. This seemed to provide a helpful transition space from the regressive states of therapy into the next part of her day. It is important to recognize, however, that this singing of goodbye only began in the *second year* of our work. Prior to this, Lily would have struggled immensely if such a firm and formalized ending had been imposed by me. This is why we need to be attachment informed in our work, and not rely solely on our own music therapy training and habits of practice.

Hospitalization and intimations of early abandonment

In 2016–2018 Lily experienced multiple hospitalizations which re-traumatized her in the extreme. She returned to playing out angry frustrations in her music. Overarching themes from earlier work emerged. Instruments became solely objects to hold her anger. As havoc was wreaked on her body that she could not make sense of, she in turn wreaked havoc in the music therapy room. Lily felt she needed once more to defend herself emotionally (as she had as a baby) and become extremely well self-contained again. She regressed from where it seemed we had reached, and demonstrated renewed refusal to allow others in.

Each hospital admission resonated with Lily's embodied memories of being a rejected baby, especially as she was abandoned in hospital and spent her earliest days and weeks there while her birth parents deliberated about relinquishment. Both I and her adoptive mother believed Lily had an emotional sense that she had been rejected because she was disabled, and that her lived experience held deep knowledge of this. Such a sense was reawakened on each admission. The impact of admissions was mediated by her secure, loving, accepting adoptive mother, but she needed music therapy too as a place to safely regress.

Sadly, Lily's physical problems worsened over the years of her music therapy, impacting on her emotional and psychological functioning. Music therapy happened in hospital whenever she was seriously ill, and was supported by hospital staff, even in the last year of her life in the high dependency unit. Necessary medical care/interventions were experienced as invasive and traumatic by Lily. She remained at risk from other serious health events (including stroke). She had seizures and wore a protective helmet (which she hated!). Her continued distress (which could only be expressed in externalized behaviours in hospital) was given voice in our music-making and singing together. I sang at such times in hospital with her about how difficult her experience was, and Lily allowed supportive vocal holding to soothe her, even sometimes sitting physically close to me, gazing at me.

As discussed in Chapter 8, many adopted children have used materials additional to musical instruments in our work. Lily engaged in much symbolic play, as these examples describe.

Symbolic play 1: baby doll 'GiGi'

Early on in music therapy, Lily began using a baby doll which she invested with symbolic significance. At times, the doll apparently represented aspects of Lily's self and she called it 'GiGi' (her pronunciation of her own name), yet at other times it was an object into which she projected her feelings about the world, revealing further aspects of her inner world functioning. Sometimes, the doll represented babies on the hospital wards Lily was on, and at others also represented her adopted (younger) sibling. Varying symbolic representations could co-exist in a single musical episode. For months, the doll's head was bashed repeatedly off the guitar, resulting in sounds I could musically hold, contain and respond to (Bion's 'alpha communications' perhaps? See Chapter 7), while simultaneously giving me a symbolic message about 'damage' being located in Lily's head, in the context of her learning disability (Cottis 2009). The 'damaged' doll also had to be repeatedly thrown away and rejected.

Towards the end of our work together, Lily's use of the doll changed dramatically. She became able to provide soothing nurture for herself using her own voice and singing, ostensibly to the doll but also to her internal baby self. Now she could tenderly and softly care for the 'baby'. 'GiGi' was sometimes wrapped in a blanket, which Lily extended around her own body while listening to me play lullabies. 'Rock-A-Bye Baby' was a favourite tune that spoke of her lived experience, but provided a frame for thinking about it safely. In hospital, 'GiGi' had to have the same procedures as Lily and often singing about these as they happened helped Lily to tolerate them. She used the doll's bottle to 'feed' herself, and such regressed states occurred at home too, supported by her adopted mother. We both viewed such regression as fundamental to Lily's reparative experience of the very early nurture she was denied. On a relational level, it also indicated that Lily was able to take goodness in from music therapy, internalizing me, and internalizing good experiences to take away.

Symbolic play 2: mummies and babies – the owl family

Lily used 'mummy' and 'baby' owl puppets in songs we co-created about mummies who could drop their babies and fly away forever. In early sessions, Lily would throw each of the babies, and then the mummy, across the room in different directions (reminiscent symbolically of her adoption experience of abandonment by birth parents). Years later, she requested that the mummy owl sang a 'finding song' as all the 'baby' owls were reunited and cared for by 'mummy'. During these times, we discussed possible fantasies and desires Lily may have about her birth mother returning to claim her, but also about how she was safe and found now and could not be stolen away from the safety and security of her adoptive placement.

Merging

Experiences of closeness and even merging with another were required before Lily could experience her separateness and individuality. Sharing an object can be a way for a child to merge with an adult in order to feel attached, in a similar way to how a mother and infant are initially merged. Lily utilized two simple long red bendy tubes (symbolically very like an umbilical cord) to physically play with feeling merged. She would sing into one end, instructing me to hold the other end to my ear. Then I would be instructed to similarly vocalize while she listened to me. Finally, both of us had to sing into the tube at the same time. We literally shared and exchanged sounds, vocalizations and even our breath. Such a merged way of being together was reminiscent again of the early life experiences Lily had missed out on.

At later times in the work, when Lily needed to feel matched closely, she would regress to playing very simple instruments, sitting together on the floor with me, mimicking early developmental positions. Gradually, she managed physical distancing, knowing I was no less present to her in my embodiment, and that music could offer holding in the physical space between us.

Lily loved to play the piano together from the outset of our work, first with her sitting on my lap, playing in the same rhythm and key. Out of this play emerged a different music, which became able to contain two distinct voices. Lily requested that I sat at the opposite end of the keyboard from her, where she could see and feel my embodied presence. She recognized when I followed her dynamic and tempo, enjoying this, and later developed this to enjoying piano duets. This shift grew from my following her lead, to playing relationally, with each of us equal partners, both hearing and responding to (and thereby being affected by) the other.

Rhythm

Rhythm developed enormously over the years of work, until Lily became able to match my pulse and share rhythms which I initiated, and was not threatened if I joined a beat she initiated. She let me provide a slow, steady beat for her to improvise over, allowing for musical holding and sustaining, within which she could create. As we experimented in free improvisation, Lily was far more able to tolerate the 'other'. We became two people relating musically, rather than her simply using me as an object to respond to her musical demands.

Anger and 'badness'

Chapter 3 described how children relinquished for adoption at birth feel that *they* somehow must be very bad inside to have been rejected. Such a belief keeps the birth parents 'good' and can act as a defence to thinking about the realities of being abandoned. Lily used the dragon puppet to represent her 'badness', enacted in improvisations. Dragon would roar and bare his teeth and Lily would gleefully say 'teeth!' to me. Dragon would (quite gently) attack me (a step removed from her attacking me). Dragon would invite play, but reject it by growling in displeasure. Similar behaviours, if demonstrated in Lily's classroom, resulted in her being reprimanded, and she would enter sessions describing herself as 'bad'. She needed to know that in music therapy she could express 'bad' things, such as hatred and anger, but not be rejected as a 'bad self'. At the end of play, Lily always kissed dragon, symbolically indicating that although dragon may represent and contain difficult material, he was still loveable.

Over time, Lily became able to more directly own her emotions and play them out musically. She would drop cymbals to the floor, enjoying the loud 'crash', and would ask me to play incredibly loudly for her on piano. As I did so, she vocalized non-verbally but furiously, articulating valid anger, rage and frustration. She would search out sounds echoing feeling states, using the thunder drum for example. We co-created a song enabling her to safely express anger: 'When she's cross, and when she's angry, we will keep her safe, safe, safe.' The musical frame provided a 'soundtrack' for difficult emotions and memories to be worked through. As Lily became more securely attached, she risked revealing a more real, whole sense of self, rather than one which was constantly having to be mediated for others.

What can be learned from Lily?

Lily's case study demonstrates clearly how music therapy might offer a means of significant relational reparation and growth in terms of allowing a self to make meaningful attachments with others. Significant developmental progress was made (as we replayed developmental milestones) but Lily also needed developmental regressions, which we learn have value too. We cannot assume a linear journey through music therapy for adoptees. As trauma re-emerged repeatedly, Lily's un-worded vocalizations contained great emotion, her huge declamatory singing expressing her emotional commitment. We cannot know 'what' is happening at such times, but wordless communications can be expressions of pre-linguistic material. Interestingly, her verbal language did develop more as she experimented with singing/vocalizing, but this was never framed as an 'aim' or 'goal'. Perhaps more meaningfully in terms of adoption, her adopted mother also utilized singing in other contexts. Sung language seemed to be easier than spoken for accessing difficult, early, emotion-laden material.

We can learn from Lily that if we are truly client-led, then 'progress' in adoption work is about a spiralling journey. There were times when, in regressive states, it appeared she might be perceived as 'going backwards', but she never regressed to precisely the place she was at before. Rather, she moved onwards, in a circling, repeating motion which seemed to provide a necessary sense of repetition and rhythm to life that her lived experience of adoption had denied her. We can learn from the contact with Lily's adopted mother the importance of authentically sharing ongoing concerns as well as positive developments within the adoptive family. Most importantly, we can learn the significance of witnessing over and over the traumatic nature of lived experience, so we can offer an accepting maternal presence (regardless of the music therapist's gender) which has been denied to adoptees in early life. Lily's lived experience in music therapy shows that, as an adoptee comes to trust a reparative therapeutic relationship, feeling contained and held musically, they might experiment with new ways of relating which can be taken out into the rest of life to play with.

Chapter 11

Co-Constructing Future Practice with the Adoption Community

At the close of this book, I offer some suggestions for how music therapy might be co-constructed for the future, as we listen to the lived experience of the adoption community in order to practice in genuinely needs-led ways. In the current socio-political context, music therapists need to articulate their voice and speak up for the sorts of work our clients with lived experience of adoption really need and for which they are calling. Our voice should be articulated alongside theirs, and developed from our experiences of working within the adoption community if we are to avoid simply shaping music therapy to fit funding demands. It is my hope that, in spite of a climate of austerity leading to reduced resources, we can persevere with robust well-researched and client-led practice.

Can we argue coherently as music therapists for a relational therapy for adoptees in contexts that are frequently driven by market forces?

An evaluation of the Adoption Support Fund (The Tavistock Institute for Human Rights 2017) refers explicitly to the 'market' of post-adoption support. It is clear that support needs are being construed in the context of a free-market economy that operates more broadly across health and social care. There are currently 11 types of therapeutic support ('providers') listed on the ASF website that the fund will pay for (although it states it is not restricted to these). Music therapy, then, faces what might be perceived as competition from other therapies, and potentially music therapists could find themselves having to articulate *why* music therapy specifically should be chosen over any other therapy. It is my hope, however, that as music therapists we do not have to view our work as being in competition with others, and instead can focus on working with those families who we believe will most likely benefit specifically from a musical modality. Future research may be able to clarify how to identify such families. Sometimes I will suggest to a family seeking music therapy that another therapy type may in fact be best for them. There is certainly enough need being expressed for all providers to work with.

All creative therapies are listed together as one such therapeutic support and within this subcategory only music therapy and art therapy are currently specifically identified and listed. The definition of what music therapy might 'do' for adoptive families requesting support, however, is rather constructed as aims and goals, as described here: 'It can help to increase concentration and attention skills, improve family and social relationships, and increase a child's confidence'. Unfortunately, we cannot guarantee any of this in our work and certainly in my own experience I have found that some situations will get worse before they get better, especially as adoptees express trauma over again. The language on the ASF website describes 'finding ways of *dealing* with feelings of loss, frustration, emotional trauma'. Such language constructs adopted people's emotional lives as something to be 'dealt with' and does not acknowledge the lifelong nature of the adoption trajectory, and how the effects of trauma can re-emerge rather than being once-and-for-all 'dealt' with.

Adult adoptees have identified that a more helpful way of thinking about their adoption journey is to talk about ways of 'managing' the loss that endures. So, perhaps a 'good outcome' might mean that an adoptee is more able to integrate their trauma into life, and to make a new sense of it. Such a sense can lead through shame and attendant emotions of guilt and badness, to a place of recognition of the sad realities and losses that lead to adoption, but which are not the fault of anyone, least of all the adoptee. Adoptive families themselves are requesting access to *lifelong* supports that can be accessed at varying times, especially at transitions that they know are likely to raise difficulties, throughout family life.

Relational psychoanalysis (which informs my approach and has in turn influenced a stance known as 'relational music therapy') highlights 'an intersubjective perspective, indicating how therapeutic change may come about through non-verbal processes at the micro level' (Trondalen 2016, p.ix). Such processes involve 'empathy, intimacy, mutuality, and relationship'. Client and music therapist relate to each other in fundamentally human ways. Trondalen continues that 'all human beings are always more than – semper major – what meets the eye…What we perform in life – musically, biologically, socially, or spiritually – does not disclose the depths in our existence.' The lived experience of being adopted begins from the most fundamental place of becoming human – our birth. Adoptees, who are at the forefront of petitioning and advocating for supportive therapeutic relationships to enable them to make sense of their adoptions, do not view themselves as 'purchasers' in a system. They request therapies that can engage with relevance and meaning to their lived experience and, in essence, to their humanity. In collaboration with the community that we work within, I believe it is possible, still, to construct ways of working that are meaningful and truly engaged with the reality of the lives of those with whom we are privileged to engage.

But how do we argue for the long-term music therapy work that this book advocates, in a culture that often demands instant 'results'?

The evaluation of the ASF (The Tavistock Institute for Human Rights 2017, p.11) states that in the future 'processes should ensure the quality and depth of assessments are not sacrificed by the need to respond to increased demand'. In all music therapy work, there can be pressures to reduce the length of our involvement with a child, adult or family, and often these pressures are structured in a context of many other clients presenting with many more needs. The evaluation report on the ASF does, however, seem to contain within it some hope for us continuing to engage in the necessary long-term work adoption so often requires. If we offer 'quality and depth' at the point of *assessing* therapeutic need, then the needs that we find arising from such assessment should be fully described.

Of course, if it is appropriate and possible to complete a piece of work within six weeks, then we will do so. However, I have yet to work with an adoption case that presents with issues that are going to be made sense of in the short term. Also, incidentally, I have never heard any referring agency ever offer a rationale for short-term work. The majority of adoption specialist professionals (social workers in post-adoption support etc.) are extremely familiar with the nature of attachment and trauma-informed work. Often by the time a family is referred to music therapy they will have run the gamut of other support and will frequently be in desperate positions, even with the possibility of the adoption breaking down. At a point in a family's trajectory when there seems to be little hope, services are more prepared to accept that music therapy will need time.

I will usually state in my pre-assessment discussions with referrers/families that a *minimum* of a year of work will be required, and often as much as three years. Recognition among all who work in adoption and who are managing the longevity of trauma presentations means that a rationale for long-term work has been accepted. The issues we are working with as music therapists in adoption are almost inevitably going to be complex and deeply entrenched. It is therefore incumbent on us to engage with each family in ways that truly are capable of meeting their expressed needs and presenting difficulties, and probably other needs that are not yet known. I would suggest that it is in fact an ethical and moral imperative that we remain engaged while the family needs us, because a family that we are actively involved in working with becomes our professional responsibility to serve properly. We can experience the pressure of 'other' families and demands and needs, but other families are not 'our' clients. We are responsible for working with our current clients and advocating for their continuing therapy needs if these are indicated. When we then are able to end work with families, we hope they will go on to experience improved relating, and the risk of breakdown will be avoided.

Certainly, as my own practice has developed in this way, the 'evidence' has been there in lived realities that families have not been disrupted. At its most pragmatic, this represents a cost saving to other agencies in health and social care. If a placement breaks down then alternative care needs to be found for children (often extremely expensive residential therapeutic placements). Some adoptees may continue to enact trauma that remains held, unconsciously, in embodied memory, and as such may re-enter other services. Therefore, a long-term therapy that engages with and addresses deep relational material can be construed as cheap! I do not see quick results in my practice, nor do I encourage others to expect them, but what is evident are much longer-term results. The adoption community can then advocate from within itself, based on experiences members have had of music therapy, and maintain good practice in collaboration with us.

Will the Adoption Support Fund (ASF) continue as a responsive source of funding, or will the huge pressure on it as a resource mean that limits are set on how much therapy can be provided?

In October 2016, the Department for Education (DfE) announced that demand for the ASF was over twice the level forecast. Clearly the government had underestimated the immense need for therapeutic support that the adoption community was articulating. Historically, families had struggled to get such support (as Chapter 4 discusses) and Michael Gove, as initiator of the fund in 2015, felt it was unfair that there was inequity on a national level. Many families interpreted Michael Gove's ideas (Gove 2012) and subsequent policies regarding adoption as intimating that all that children (who were seen to be languishing in care) needed was to be loved, in a familial context. This idea failed to take into account the voices from the lived experience of parents who, whilst continuing to offer a loving family home, still knew immense struggles and heartache. This was inexplicable if love alone was supposed to heal their adopted children. Little attention had been paid in Gove's setting up of the ASF to what was known about the tentacles of trauma that can stretch into adoptive family life, and the huge pressures these can bring. In an outpouring of demand on the ASF, however, families articulated their need…and there were many of them.

Adoptive families have been vocal and articulated the sorts of issues they are managing, in the private realm of the family, and which are therefore often hidden from wider society. Families who face little understanding outside the adoption community are subject to well-meaning people (sometimes including professionals) who offer advice and behaviour management that is ineffectual when dealing with the needs this book has described. The adoption community is itself well informed about trauma and attachment, and families can talk about the difficulties they are having in these terms. Parents will often ring me to discuss referring for music therapy via the ASF/local authority and clearly articulate their children's presentations sympathetically and with awareness. The adoption community is clear about what sort of help it needs and desires, and what this should look like. To date, the ASF has been timely in its response to many requests and I have never yet had an application turned down. Also, requests by myself, as a music therapist, to continue work beyond the first initial time limit have also been agreed. Such requests can be articulated, for example, in reports that may be written, where a child's engagement with a non-verbal medium can be evaluated. If a continued need for therapy can be described, and an informed rationale offered, therapy will carry on being funded. We can be our own advocates in this sense, and use the systems we function within to make our case, based on our training and research.

However, despite increased funding to attempt to deal with demand, the ASF on its own website stated it had been 'forced' to take action to limit access to the fund. The 'fair access limit' of £5000 per child was introduced as well as the match-funding approach (whereby local authorities share the cost of support over the fair access limit). Access to match-funding is based on evidence of high risk of adoption breakdown, and some families have described needing to say that they fear their adoption might break down in order to access funding. This is extremely problematic as, in stating such a possibility, families may become subject to scrutiny and some have even found themselves subject to unrequested interventions, even entering safeguarding situations.

In December 2018, the DfE increased funding by an additional £12 million, taking the totals for 2018/19 and 2019/20 to £37 million and £40 million respectively. At the time of writing the government have committed some funding for the 2021–22 financial year. The future of funding is unclear, but we know that the adoption community is a force which continues to petition for the needs of its members, and will not simply re-absorb identified needs for therapeutic support into family life. As music therapists, we need to know the needs of our client base from the lived experience of its members in order to be able to argue cogently for them.

How might we share aspects of our work without compromising clients in a 'PR' exercise?

Music therapy in the adoption contexts I have described throughout this book is something that takes place in a private setting, if we follow basic principles of working psychoanalytically, where the 'frame' is at the centre of all we do. This means we meet every week, at the same time, in the same place, with the individuals we work with. The room is private and confidential, and therefore safe. In such a place, there exists permission for thoughts and behaviours that might not be deemed 'acceptable' or 'appropriate' elsewhere. The space that is thus created and offered can contain the worst fears parents might have of adoption breakdown, or indeed their hopes that this might occur when things are feeling desperate. It can hold the trauma and attachment communications of children who are functioning with internal world states that might require regression. It can enable truth to be spoken from one family member to another as unconscious material painfully is revealed.

What happens, then, in those week-on-week meetings, and in the playing of music and embodied relating together, remains private. It is absolutely imperative, if utilizing the approach that I describe in this book, that such a frame is in place to contain the work. As we have seen, adoptees will have issues around containment which requires safe structure and boundaries to enable the depth of work necessary. This is not something that is happening and exists out in the public domain. Models of 'community music therapy' then, for example, would not offer the sufficient containment that adoption work requires, and it is the nature of the client's needs and presentation that must inform the approach we adopt.

Unless you are part of the adoption community, you may rarely hear about it. And aspects of what 'goes on' in therapy cannot easily be described and talked about with others. This is problematic when we are required to share work in order to explain its use and function to other professionals, or indeed to families themselves. At the point of requesting music therapy, families may have little real sense of what it is all about. To enable us to share work, it is once again imperative that we are embedded within the adoption community. Many families we work with are extremely able and competent to talk about their experiences, and to state how valuable they have personally found music therapy. We may need to gently protect families who wish to do so, in order for them not to become over-exposed, or to share beyond a level they feel comfortable with. However, families themselves are best placed to let others know what it is music therapists do. Adopters at the point of adoption are connected up with other adopters. Local adoption support groups exist, run by the community and for the community. The local authority and other charitable adoption agencies regularly run family days for adoptive families who have been through their systems. Families develop friendships and talk about their experiences. In these ways, news of the value of music therapy has spread. We might also need to present our work in the public domain and need to find ways (ideally jointly with families) of doing so. My own motivation for doing research was to find a way to explain and academically validate the approach that I evolved. Similarly, writing about our work can enable others to access it (as is the hope and intent of this book). We can write and present for conferences both inside and outside music therapy, and raise awareness of our profession within the professional world of adoption.

Which narratives might now construct a transition to the future?

I hope that this book has demonstrated above all that if we want to work as music therapists in adoption, our work must first and foremost be led by the adoption community – a community that has learned and continues to be informed by the lived experience of its members.

To learn from the adoption community ourselves means setting aside perhaps some of our professional power. It means adopting a 'not knowing' stance and becoming curious about what we see presented. It means dropping our preconceived ideas and theories, and perhaps returning to training or further study in order to engage in our own sense-making. It means walking into each new assessment and recognizing that we may meet something we have never met before. As Aldridge (1996) recognizes, 'relational experiences through music frame and support our ongoing creative processes, activities invested with that vital quality of hope' (p.199). By acknowledging we have much to learn ourselves, we are actually participating in our own development.

There are voices of adult adoptees in the adoption literature who have experienced various therapeutic interventions and are able to talk about what has been helpful (and, equally, what has not). One study of lived experience (Mangilit *et al.* 2013) states that adopted individuals expressed a 'lack of feelings of belonginess from being raised by their adoptive parents that led them to adjust in different ways' (p.199). If we know that this 'lack of feeling' (or, in another description that has been used throughout this book, the 'primal wound' of Verrier 1993) has impacted on adjustment through life, we can be better placed to work now with children who are currently living with such lack. When lack and loss can be felt, known and contained, then future life might be adjusted to in different ways. However, we need to be open to criticism of how we work, and indeed to working with the enactments of both parents and children who have been subject to huge distress, and as such may have much to be very angry about.

When we work with lived experience we redefine clients as experts in their own lives. Adoptees and their families have lived themselves with the outworking of trauma and attachment difficulties and can teach us much about what that actually feels like. As feeling is the main referent of our work, this is valuable information. At the same time, though, of course it is imperative that we develop our own knowledge, practice, and (the most useful tool for this work) our self. Although I have at times myself been referred to as an 'expert' in adoption matters, I do not consider this a helpful term. Families are experts, and we, as professional people working in the adoption community and possibly sharing lived experience with it, are learning our expertise. This is why this book does not prescribe a model for the approach I use, but instead offers an invitation to you, the reader, to return to your own music therapy work space and think about what might 'fit'…and to jettison what does not…and explore what else is needed.

My own journey of learning about how it might be possible to work as a music therapist within adoption has itself not been linear. I have drawn on previous training prior to music therapy, as well as my own psychoanalytic music therapy training. To this has been added knowledge from the most useful bodies of theory that I have found to date, namely contemporary attachment theory, trauma-informed theory, embodied theory and relational psychoanalysis. I have been fortunate to study for my PhD at a university that encourages interdisciplinary work, and which has caused me to think about my life as a music therapist from multiple perspectives. I certainly therefore second Trondalen's (2016) proposal that 'all these perspectives are basic to understanding the process of forming our identity, or who we are as human beings. Identity is not a fixed item but an ongoing process.' (p.142) Fortunately, as Trondalen (2016, p.4, citing Bonde 2015 and Ruud 2016) also later says, 'the music therapy landscape is not fixed but constantly in motion…with the lived experience at the forefront'. It is my hope that the reader is encouraged by this book, and especially by the narratives of adopted people and their families existing within it, to deepen their listening to the lived experiences of adoption, and through so doing forge a robust yet human music therapy practice for adoption.

Appendix 1

Addresses of useful contacts for music therapy/adoptions

British Association for Music Therapy
24–27 White Lion Street
London
N1 9PD
020 7837 6100
www.bamt.org

Coram BAAF (successor to the British Association for Adoption and Fostering)
Coram Campus
41 Brunswick Square
London
WC1N 1AZ
020 7520 0300
www.corambaaf.org.uk

Additional training in attachment theory

The Association for Psychological Therapies
The Dower House
Thurnby
Leicestershire
LE7 9PH
0116 241 8331
www.apt.ac

The John Bowlby Training Centre
1 Highbury Crescent
London
N5 1RN
020 7700 5070
https://thebowlbycentre.org.uk

Attachment in the Early Years with The Open University
The Open University
PO Box 197
Milton Keynes
MK7 6BJ
0300 303 5303
www.open.edu/openlearn

Attachment in Psychotherapy
Confer
21 California
Woodbridge
IP12 4DE
020 7535 7595
www.confer.uk.com

Beacon House
AD5 Littlehampton Marina
Ferry Road
Littlehampton
BN17 5DS
01243 219900
https://beaconhouse.org.uk

Appendix 2

This is the text from a leaflet describing music therapy in adoption that is available free on the British Association for Music Therapy website (www.bamt.org).

British Association for Music Therapy

The British Association for Music Therapy (BAMT) is the professional body representing music therapy and music therapists in the UK. It is a source of information, support and involvement for the general public, and acts as a voice for those who could benefit from music therapy and those who provide music therapy.

What is music therapy?

As human beings, music plays a fundamental role in our identity, culture, heritage and spiritual beliefs. It is a powerful medium that can affect us all deeply. In music therapy, music therapists draw on the innate qualities of music to support people of all ages and abilities and at all stages of life; from helping new born babies develop healthy bonds with their parents, to offering vital, sensitive and compassionate palliative care at the end of life.

Everyone has the ability to respond to music, and music therapy uses this connection to facilitate positive changes in emotional wellbeing and communication through the engagement in live musical interaction between client and therapist. It can help develop and facilitate communication skills, improve self-confidence and independence, enhance self-awareness and awareness of others, improve concentration and attention skills.

Central to how music therapy works is the therapeutic relationship that is established and developed, through engagement in live musical interaction and play between a therapist and client. A wide range of musical styles and instruments can be used, including the voice, and the music is often improvised. Using music in this way enables clients to create their own unique musical language in which to explore and connect with the world and express themselves.

Music therapy is an established clinical intervention, which is delivered by HCPC registered music therapists to help people whose lives have been affected by injury, illness or disability through supporting their psychological, emotional, cognitive, physical, communicative and social needs.

Music therapy and adoption – supporting attachment and healthy relationships

Adoption is currently preferred as a new family form for removed children to grow up in, where they can find stability, certainty, security and love.

Statistics show that 70% of children adopted in the UK have experienced neglect and abuse. Early trauma can result in high stress levels in infancy which impacts on the brain, nervous system and physiological development, undermining a child's capacity to form attachments. Because of this, adoptees may be diagnosed with attachment disorders and adoptive parents may struggle with secondary traumatization, impacted on by parenting adopted children.

Evidence shows that music therapy is a therapeutic modality that helps children to heal and re-attach. Adopters might also need their own therapeutic support in order to be able to parent therapeutically.

Sam was 14 when he was referred to therapy because of his behavioural difficulties after his distraught adoptive parents had requested that he go back into care.

Sam worked on his own with his therapist at first, who identified the unconscious motivations which caused him to jeopardize new relationships.

In spontaneous song, Sam found a safe place to re-live abuse and trauma experiences he had endured in his birth family, which previously were expressed in hyperarousal and flashbacks.

Sam eventually asked if his adoptive mother could attend sessions too. Within the safety of the musical relationship, Sam could regress and on one occasion played the xylophone like a toddler. His mum was able to cuddle him and acknowledge the loss of relationship in his earliest years. She also gained insight into why Sam may act in negative ways, which destroyed all the good and love they wanted to offer him. These music therapy sessions contributed to Sam remaining with his adoptive family.

Scientific research of the brain shows that engaging in therapy can help the brain develop new neural pathways. This is known as 'neuroplasticity'. Music therapy possesses specific qualities, which are often called 'communicative musicality'. The elements of rhythm and repetition within music are similar to the ebb and flow of the rhythms in early life relationships. Adopted children miss out on these. Working in moments of free, improvisatory therapeutic relationships, music therapists can open up attachment processes and enable an understanding of children's attachment styles.

Music therapy can meet and reflect awful trauma experiences and mirror painful emotions safely. It can enable processing and assimilation of the emotional impact of traumatic experience. By musically relating with a therapist, a child might engage in a new 'dance' of attunement, where early intuitive emotional communication can be made evident. In this experience of being held in the minds and hearts of new carers, reparation may begin.

Currently provision of music therapy for adopted children and adopters is uneven across the UK and families in need of therapeutic support are not always able to access the support they need. Many more could benefit from music therapy if services were expanded.

References

Ainsworth, M.D.S., Blehar, M.C., Waters, E. and Wall, S. (1978). *Patterns Of Attachment*. Hillsdale, New Jersey. Lawrence Erlbaum Associates.

Alaane, S. (2016) *Music Psychotherapy with Refugee Survivors of Torture*. Helsinki, Finland: Picaset Oy.

Aldridge, D. (1996) *Music Therapy Research and Practice in Medicine: From out of the Silence*. London: Jessica Kingsley Publishers.

Austin, D. (2009) *The Theory and Practice of Vocal Psychotherapy*. London: Jessica Kingsley Publishers.

Beebe, B. and Lachmann, F.M. (2002) *Infant Research and Adult Treatment: Co-Constructing Interactions*. London: Analytic Press.

Bettelheim, B. (1950) *Love Is Not Enough*. New York, NY: Collier Books, The Macmillan Company.

Bion, W. (1959) 'Attacks on linking.' *International Journal of Psychoanalysis*, 40(5–6), 308.

Bion, W. (1962/1984) *Learning from Experience*. London: Karnac.

Bion, W. (1963) *Elements of Psychoanalysis*. London: Heinemann.

Bjorkland, S. (2014) 'How Betty and Vincent Became Sally and Scott.' In S. Kuchuck, *Clinical Implications of the Psychoanalyst's Life Experience: When the Personal Becomes Professional*. Hove: Routledge.

Bonde, L.O. (2015) 'The current state of music therapy theory?' *Nordic Journal of Music Therapy*, 24(2), 167–175.

Bowlby, J. (1953) *Child Care and the Growth of Love*. London: Harmondsworth, Penguin.

Bowlby, J. (1998) *A Secure Base: Clinical Applications of Attachment Theory*. London: Routledge.

Bridge, C. and Swindells, H. (2003) *Adoption: The Modern Law*. Bristol: Jordan Publishing.

British Association for Adoption and Fostering (2011) 'Taking The Next Step: Enquries To National Adoption Week One Year On.' *Journal of Adoption and Fostering*. 935(1).

Cairnes, K. (2002) *Attachment, Trauma, and Resilience: Therapeutic Caring for Children*. London: British Association for Adoption and Fostering.

Carter, C.S. (1998) 'Neuroendocrine perspectives on social attachment and love.' *Psychoneuroendocrinology*, 23, 819–835.

Cottis, T. (ed.) (2009) *Intellectual Disability, Trauma and Psychotherapy*. Hove: Routledge.

Cozolino, L. (2006) *The Neuroscience of Human Relationships: Attachment and the Developing Brain*. London and New York, NY: W.W. Norton.

De Waal, F. (2012) 'The antiquity of empathy.' *Science*, 336(6083), 874–876.

Delaney, R. (1998) *Fostering Changes: Treating Attachment Disordered Children*. Oklahoma City, OK: Wood Barnes Publishing.

Dimigen, G., Del Priore, C., Butler, S., Evans, S., Ferguson, L. and Swan, M. (1999) 'Psychiatric disorder among children at time of entering local authority care: Questionnaire survey.' *British Medical Journal*, 319, 675.

Driver, C. (ed.) (2013) *Being and Relating in Psychotherapy: Ontology and Therapeutic Practice*. London: Palgrave Macmillan.

Eigen, M. (2014) *The Birth Of Experience*. New York. Routledge.

Elias, L. (2018). *Department for Education: Adoption Reform Update: Spring 2018*. www.gov.uk/dfe (accessed 26 November 2020).

Eliot, T.S. (1943) *Four Quartets*. New York, NY: Harcourt.

Fahlberg, V. (1994) *A Child's Journey Through Placement*. London: British Association for Adoption and Fostering.

Federici-Nebbiosi, S. and Nebbiosi, G. (2012) 'The experience of another body on our body in psychoanalysis: Commentary on paper by Jon Sletvold.' *Psychoanalytic Dialogues*, 22, 430–436.

Fisher, P.A and Chamberlain, P. (2000) 'Multidimensional treatment foster care: A programme for intensive parenting, family support, and skill building.' *Journal of Emotional and Behavioural Disorders*, 8(3), 155–165.

Fosha, D. (2003) 'Dyadic Regulation and Experiential Work with Emotion and Relatedness.' In M.F. Solomon and D.J. Siegel (eds), *Healing Trauma, Attachment, Mind, Body and Brain*. New York, NY: W.W. Norton.

Freud, S. (1920/2003) *Beyond the Pleasure Principle: And Other Writings*. London: Penguin Classics.

Freud, S. (1922) *Group Psychology and the Analysis of the Ego*. New York, NY: Boni & Liveright.

Gallese, V. (2005) 'Embodied simulation: From neurons to phenomenal experience.' *Phenomenology and the Cognitive Sciences*, 4, 23–48.

Gallese, V. and Ammaniti, M. (2013) *The Birth of Intersubjectivity: Psychodynamics, Neurobiology, and The Self*. New York, NY: W.W. Norton.

Geltner, P. (2012) *Emotional Communication: Countertransference Analysis and the Use of Feeling in Psychoanalytic Technique*. New York, NY: Routledge.

Glassman, N. and Botticelli, S. (2014) 'Perspectives on Gay Fatherhood: Emotional Legacies and Clinical Reverberations.' In S. Kuchuck, *Clinical Implications of the Psychoanalyst's Life Experience: When the Personal Becomes Professional*. Hove: Routledge.

Gold, K. (2016) Personal communication. Cambridge.

Gove, M. (2012) Speech on adoption. Department for Education. Retrieved from www.gov.uk/government/speeches/michael-gove-speech-on-adoption.

Gravestock, J. (2012) 'Adoption music therapy'. Paper presented for Anglia Ruskin Music Therapy Conference, November 2012, Cambridge.

Gravestock, J. (2018) 'Attachment-based, relational, psychoanalytic music therapy: The significance of musical moments of attunement with adoptees after trauma, and how this may influence broader reparation with attachments.' *Attachment*, 12(2), 147.

Gravestock, J. (2019a) 'Evolving a Contemporary Psychoanalytically Informed Relational Music Therapy with Children with High Functioning Autism in Specialist School Placements.' In H. Dunn, E. Coombes, E. Maclean, H. Mottram and J. Nugent (eds), *Music Therapy and Autism Across the Life Span: A Spectrum of Approaches*. London: Jessica Kingsley Publishers.

Gravestock, J. (2019b) *Micro moments of attunement with children/young adults of adoptive families, receiving attachment based, relational music therapy, and the significance of therapeutic attunement with these clients (who have trauma experience prior to placement). An explorative multiple case study research*. Unpublished PhD thesis. Sheffield University.

Greenwood, H. (2011) Long term individual art psychotherapy: Art for art's sake: The effect of early relational trauma. *Journal of the British Association of Art Therapists*, 16(1), 41–51.

The Guardian (2012). Henderson. *I Wanted to Kill Her*. P.9, 01/11/12.

Hart, A. and Lucock, B. (2004) *Developing Adoption Support and Therapy: New Approaches for Practice*. London. Jessica Kingsley Publishers.

Heidegger, M. (1959) 'On the Way to Language'. In M. Heidegger, *Gesamtausgabe*. Vol. 12. Werne, Germany: Verlag Vittorio Klostermann.

Heidegger, M., Macquarrie, J. and Robinson, E. (1927/1962) *Being and Time*. Malden, MA: Blackwell.

Howe, D. and Fearnley, S. (1999) 'Disorders of attachment and attachment therapy.' *Adoption and Fostering*, 23(2), 19–30.

Hughes, D. (1997) *Facilitating Developmental Attachment: The Road to Recovery and Behavioural Change in Foster and Adopted Children*. Northval, NJ: Aronson.

Jung, C.J. (1946/1983) *The Psychology of the Transference*. Hove: Routledge.

Kay, J. (1991) *The Adoption Papers*. Hexham: Bloodaxe.

Knox, J. (2011) *Self-Agency in Psychotherapy: Attachment, Autonomy and Intimacy*. New York, NY and London: W.W. Norton.

Kuchuck, S. (2014) *Clinical Implications of the Psychoanalyst's Life Experience: When the Personal Becomes Professional*. Hove: Routledge.

Lakoff, G. (1987) *Women, Fire, and Dangerous Things: What Categories Reveal about the Mind*. Chicago, IL: University of Chicago Press.

Loewald, H. (1980) 'Primary Process, Secondary Process, and Language.' In *Papers on Psychoanalysis*. New Haven, CT: Yale University Press.

Love, H. (2007) *Feeling Backward: Loss and the Politics of Queer History*. Cambridge, MA: Harvard University Press.

Mangilit, K.J., Puno, M.A., Valoroso, M. and Castroverde, A. (2013) *Sa Likod Ng Pagtanggap: The Lived Experience of Adopted Individuals*. Princesa City, Philippines: Palawan State University Psychology Society Publications.

Marks-Tarlow, T. (2008) *Psyche's Veil: Psychotherapy, Fractals and Complexity*. Hove: Routledge.

McCann, J., James, A., Wilson, S. and Dunn, G. (1996) 'Prevalence of psychiatric disorders in young people in the care system'. *British Medical Journal*, 313, 1529–1530.

Merleau-Ponty, M. (1945/1965) *Phenomenology of Perception*. Paris, France: Gallimard.

Nebbiosi, G. and Federici-Nebbiosi, S. (2008) '"We" Got Rhythm.' In F.S. Anderson (ed.), *Bodies in Treatment: The Unspoken Dimension*. New York, NY: Analytic Press.

Nordoff, P. and Robbins, C. (1971) *Therapy in Music for Handicapped Children*. Dallas, TX: Barcelona Publishers.

Ogden, T. (1992) *The Primitive Edge of Experience*. London: Routledge.

Pavlicevic, M. (1997) *Music Therapy in Context: Music, Meaning and Relationship*. London: Jessica Kingsley Publishers.

Phillips, A. (2007) *Winnicott*. London: Penguin.

Reich, W. (1949/1972) *Character Analysis* (3rd edn). V.R. Carfagno (Trans). New York, NY: Farrar, Strauss and Giroux.

Robarts, J. (2014) 'Music Therapy with Children with Developmental Trauma Disorder.' In C. Malchiodi and D. Crenshaw (eds), *Creative Arts and Play Therapy for Attachment Problems*. New York, NY: Guilford Press.

Rose, G.J. (2004) *Between Couch and Piano: Psychoanalysis, Music, Art and Neuroscience*. Hove: Brunner-Routledge.

Rothschild, B. (2000) *The Body Remembers: The Psychophysiology of Trauma and Trauma Treatment*. New York, NY: W.W. Norton.

Ruud, E. (2016) 'The Future of Theory in Music Therapy.' In C. Dileo (ed.), *Envisioning the Future of Music Therapy*. Philadelphia, PA: Temple University.

Salkeld, C. (2008) 'Music Therapy After Adoption; The Role of Music Therapy in Developing Secure Attachment in Adopted Children.' In A. Oldfield and C. Flower (eds), *Music Therapy with Children and Their Families*. London: Jessica Kingsley Publishers.

Schore, A. (1994) *Affect Regulation and the Origin of the Self: The Neurobiology of Emotional Development*. New York, NY: W.W. Norton.

Siegel, D. (2006) 'The Mindful Brain: Reflection and Attunement.' In D. Siegel, *The Cultivation of Well Being*. New York, NY: W.W. Norton.

Siegel, D. and Solomon, M. (2013) *Healing Moments in Psychotherapy*. London and New York, NY: W.W. Norton.

Sills, F. (2008) *Being and Becoming: Psychodynamics, Buddhism, and the Origins of Selfhood*. Berkeley, CA: North Atlantic Books.

Sletvold, J. (2014) *The Embodied Analyst: From Freud and Reich to Relationality*. Hove: Routledge.

Stern, D. (1977) *The First Relationship: Infant and Mother*. London and Cambridge, MA: Karnac.

Stern, D. (1985) *The Interpersonal World of the Infant: A View From Psychoanalysis and Developmental Psychology*. New York, NY: Basic Books.

Stern, D. (1994) 'One way to build a clinically relevant baby'. *Infant Mental Health Journal*, 15(1), 9–25.

Stern, D. (1995) *The Motherhood Constellation: A United View of Parent-Infant Psychotherapy*. London: Karnac.

Stern, D. (1998) *The Interpersonal World of the Infant*. London: Karnac.
Stern, D. (2004) *The Present Moment in Psychotherapy and Everyday Life*. New York, NY: W.W. Norton.
Stern, D. (2010) *Forms of Vitality: Exploring Dynamic Experience in Psychology, the Arts, Psychotherapy, and Development*. Oxford: Oxford University Press.
Stone, B. (2017) Personal communication in person at Sheffield University.
Sutton, J. (2002) *Music, Music Therapy and Trauma: International Perspectives*. London: Jessica Kingsley Publishers.
The Tavistock Institute for Human Rights (2017) *The Evaluation of the Adoption Support Fund*. London: Department for Education.
Totton, N. (2015) *Embodied Relating: The Ground of Psychotherapy*. London: Karnac.
Trevarthen, C. (1979) 'Communication and Co-Operation in Early Infancy: A Description of Primary Intersubjectivity.' In M. Bullowa (ed.), *Before Speech: The Beginning of Human Communication*. Cambridge: Cambridge University Press.
Trevarthen, C. (2009) In C. Trevarthen and S. Malloch, *Communicative Musicality: Exploring the Base of Human Companionship*. Oxford. Oxford University Press.
Trondalen, G. (2016) *Relational Music Therapy: An Intersubjective Perspective*. Dallas, TX: Barcelona Publishers.
Tronick, E. (2007) *The Neurobehavioural and Social-Emotional Development of Infants and Children*. New York, NY: W.W. Norton.
Tustin, F. (1981) *Autistic States in Children*. Hove: Routledge.
Van der Kolk, B. (2014) *The Body Keeps the Score*. London: Penguin.
Verrier, N. (1993) *The Primal Wound*. Baltimore, MD: Gateway Press.
Weick, K.E. (1995) *Sensemaking in Organisations*. Thousand Oaks, CA: Sage Publications.
Wilburg, P. (2013) *Being and Listening: Counselling, Psychoanalysis, and the Ontology of Listening*. Whitstable: New Yoga Publications.
Wilkinson, M. (2006) *Coming into Mind: The Mind-Brain Relationship: A Jungian Clinical Perspective*. London: Routledge.
Wilkinson, M. (2010) *Changing Minds in Therapy: Emotion, Attachment, Trauma and Neurobiology*. London and New York, NY: W.W. Norton.
Winnicott, D.W. (1949) 'Hate in the countertransference.' *International Journal of Psychoanalysis*, 30, 69–74.
Winnicott, D.W. (1960) 'The theory of the parent-infant relationship.' *International Journal of Psychoanalysis*, 41, 585–595.
Winnicott, D.W. (1965/1990) *The Maturational Processes and the Facilitating Environment*. London: Hogarth Press.
Winnicott, D.W. (1969) 'The use of an object.' *International Journal of Psychoanalysis*, 50: 711–716.
Winnicott, D.W. (1971) *Playing and Reality*. London: Tavistock Publications.
Winterson, J. (2011) *Why Be Happy When You Could Be Normal?* London: Jonathan Cape, Random House.
Wright, K. (2009) *Mirroring and Attunement: Self Realisation in Psychoanalysis and Art*. Hove and New York, NY: Routledge.

Subject Index

adopted children
    in adoption process 48–9, 50–2
    crisis in adoptions 127–8, 131–4
    music playing with 116–17
    transitional periods 94–5
    trauma in music therapy 144–6
Adoption and Children Act (2002) 52
adoption community
    co-constructing future with 195–204
    first steps in music therapy 22–4
    lived experience impact 20–1
    as network 15–16
    and referral to music therapy 93–106
    relevance of music therapy to 29–44
    self-referring 124–7
adoption panels
    in adoption process 48–50, 51, 52, 53, 54
    and attachment theory 62
Adoption Papers, The (Kay) 20
adoption process
    adopted children in 48–9, 50–2
    adoption panels in 48–50, 51, 52, 53, 54
    adoptive parents in 49–50, 53–4
    birth parents in 49
    case vignettes 55–6
    crisis in adoptions 56–60
    development of 45–50
    and later life outcomes 54–6
Adoption Support Fund (ASF) 37, 59–60, 79–82, 106, 123, 124, 129, 138, 178, 195–6, 197–8, 199–201

adoptive parents
    in adoption process 49–50, 53–4
    parenting skills for 54
    referral to music therapy 101–3, 124–7
    self-referring 124–7
    sense of shame 101–3
affect attunement 43
approaches to music therapy
    and attachment theory 61–2
    attunement in 73–7
    case vignettes 70–2, 75, 76
    containing concept 73–7
    and Daniel Stern 63–5
    development of 24–7
    and developmental theory 62–3
    and Donald Winnicott 65–73
    holding concept in 73–7
    needs-led 107–21
    and psychoanalysis 62
attachment theory 61–2, 77, 187
attunement
    case study in 184
    case vignettes 147–8
    cross-modal 147–8
    and relevance of music therapy 43–4
    in theory of music therapy 63–4, 73–7

beginning music therapy 142–4, 179–80
birth parents 49, 58–9
birthdays 95
brain science 114–15

case vignettes
    adoption process 55–6
    Adoption Support Fund
        82, 83, 87, 88, 89
    approaches to music therapy
        70–2, 75, 76
    attunement 147–8
    beginning music therapy 143–4
    crisis in adoptions 133–4, 135
    embodied music–making
        146–7, 165, 168–9
    emotional regulation 148–50
    lyrics 158–9
    maternal transference 154–5
    referral presentations 94, 98–9, 103–5
    relevance of music therapy
        38–9, 40–2
    rhythm 156–7
    self-narratives 152–3
    theory of music therapy 70–2, 75, 76
    trauma in music therapy 144–6
Children Act (2004) 46
chord circling 120–1
containing concept 73–7
crisis in adoptions
    and adoption process 56–60
    arts therapies in 129–31
    case vignettes 133–4, 135
    children as problem 131–4
    families self-referring 124–7
    impact of 127–8
    relevance of music therapy
        in 34–5, 137–9
    understanding 127–8
    witnessing 134–7
cross-modal attunement 147–8

developmental theory 62–4

embodied music–making 43–4,
    146–7, 164–9, 172–5
emotional regulation 148–51, 191–2

'going on being' sense of self 65–73, 77

holding concept 73–7

improvisational music therapy 10–11
intersubjective relating 161–76

later life outcomes
    and adoption process 54–6
    music therapy in 100–1
'Letterbox' system 59
listening
    as embodied holding process 115–16
    in music therapy 109–12
lived experiences
    case study in 177–93
    challenges to value of 22
    description of 19
    first steps in music therapy 22–4
    impact on adoption community 20–1
    of music therapists 16–17
    problems of shared 169–72
    and sense-making 21, 22–4
    value of 16, 19–20
Love Is Not Enough (Bettelheim) 55
lullabies 157–8
lyrics 158–9

maternal transference 154–6
merging 190–1
'moving along' state 64–5
music
    and brain science 114–15
    as emotional language 113–14
    features in adoption work 118–21
    as non-verbal language 29–32
    therapeutic effects of 113
music therapists
    co-constructing future with 195–204
    intersubjective relating 161–76
    and listening 109–12
    lived experience of 16–17
music therapy
    approaches to 24–7, 61–77
    beginning of 142–4, 179–80
    co-constructing future with 195–204
    embodied 43–4, 146–7, 164–9, 172–5
    facets of 9–10
    incorporating lived experiences
        and sense-making 22–4
    intersubjective 162–4
    play in 185–6, 189–90

referral to 93–106, 124–7,
    137–9, 142–3, 178
relevance of 29–44, 137–9
theory of 24–7, 61–77
musical features
    chord circling 120–1
    in needs-led music therapy 118–21
    ostinato 120–1
    repetition 120–1
    rhythm 118–20

needs-led music therapy
    and brain science 114–15
    development of 107–13
    emotional language of music 113–14
    listening in 115–16
    music playing with children 116–17
    musical features 118–21
    therapeutic effects of music 113

ostinato 120–1

play in music therapy 185–6, 189–90
Primal Wound, The (Verrier) 30, 126
psychoanalysis 62

rape 96
referrals to music therapy 93–106,
    124–7, 137–9, 142–3, 178
relational change 35–43
relevance of music therapy
    for adoptions in crisis 34–5, 137–9

and attunement 43–4
case vignettes 38–9, 40–2
in early trauma of adoption 33
as non-verbal language 29–32
relational change support 35–43
repetition 120–1
rhythm 118–20, 156–7, 191

self-narratives 151–4
sense-making 21, 22–4
shared lived experiences 169–72
silence 159–60
Stern, Daniel 63–5
Stone, Brendan 19

theory of music therapy
    and attachment theory 61–2
    attunement in 73–7
    case vignettes 70–2, 75, 76
    containing concept 73–7
    and Daniel Stern 63–5
    development of 24–7
    and developmental theory 62–3
    and Donald Winnicott 65–73
    holding concept in 73–7
    and psychoanalysis 62

*Why Be Happy When You Could
    Be Normal?* (Winterson) 51
Winnicott, Donald 65–73
witnessing 134–7

Author Index

Adoption UK 89–90
Ainsworth, M. 62
Alanne, S. 113, 114, 163, 169, 170
Aldridge, D. 203
Ammaniti, M. 144
Austin, D. 163

Beebe, B. 31, 129
Bettelheim, B. 55
Bion, W. 73–4, 76, 119, 183, 189
Bjorkland, S. 136
Bonde, I.O. 204
Botticelli, S. 134, 135
Bowlby, J. 57, 61
Bridge, C. 45, 52
British Association for Adoption and Fostering 51, 86, 90, 129, 207–9

Cairns, K. 54, 126
Carter, C.S. 35
Chamberlain, P. 138
Cottis, T. 189
Cozolino, L. 34

De Waal, F. 163
Delaney, R. 57, 103
Dimigen, G. 52
Driver, C. 161, 162

Eigen, M. 137
Eliot, T.S. 72

Fahlberg, V. 54
Fearnley, S. 54
Federici-Nebbiosi, S. 165–6
Fisher, P.A. 138
Fosha, D. 35
Freud, S. 142, 185

Gallese, V. 42, 128, 144
Geltner, P. 167
Glassman, N. 134, 135
Gold, K. 114
Gove, M. 54–5, 199
Gravestock, J. 24, 77, 108, 171, 174
Greenwood, H. 170
Guardian, The 46

Hart, A. 138
Health and Care Professionals Council (HCPC) 169
Heidegger, M. 110, 111, 136
Howe, D. 54
Hughes, D. 47, 54

Jung, C. 163

Kay, J. 20
Knox, J. 42, 105, 114, 121, 144, 180, 182
Kuchuck, S. 161

Lachmann, F.M. 31, 129
Lakoff, G. 163–4
Loewald, H. 151

Love, H. 134
Lucock, B. 138

Mangilit, K.J. 203
Marks-Tarlow, T. 163
McCann, J. 52
Merleau-Ponty, M. 110

Nebbiosi, G. 165–6
Nordoff, P. 163

Ogden, T. 32, 74

Pavlicevic, M. 183
Phillips, A. 24

Reich, W. 164
Robarts, J. 32, 120, 128, 144
Robbins, C. 163
Rose, G.J. 115
Rothschild, B. 33, 110
Ruud, E. 204

Salkeld, C. 34
Schore, A. 40, 116, 186
Siegel, D. 114, 150, 151
Sills, F. 108
Sletvold, J. 144, 147, 156, 165, 166, 167
Solomon, M. 114

Stern, D. 25, 31, 43, 63–5, 75, 76, 114, 118, 121, 129, 130, 147, 148, 173, 183
Stone, B. 21
Sutton, J. 128
Swindells, H. 45, 52

Tavistock Institute for Human Rights 195, 197
Totton, N. 31, 110
Trevarthen, C. 26, 31, 42, 128, 129, 163, 183
Trondalen, G. 197, 204
Tronick, E. 31, 129
Tustin, F. 42

Van der Kolk, B. 33, 110, 168
Verrier, N. 30, 51, 126, 182
Weick, K.E. 21

Wilburg, P. 110–12, 116
Wilkinson, M. 31–2, 34, 38, 144, 173, 183, 186
Winnicott, D. 24, 25, 27, 65–73, 74, 75, 76, 77, 113, 116, 119–20, 144, 171, 181
Winterson, J. 51, 127
Wright, K. 75